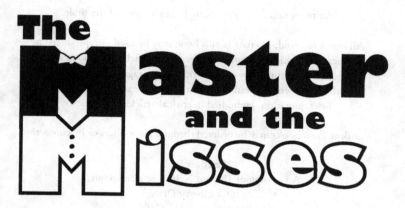

The Master and the Misses

DANCING WITH A KING

MELVIN STOKES

WestBow
PRESS®
A DIVISION OF THOMAS NELSON
& ZONDERVAN

WestBow Press books may be ordered through booksellers or by contacting:

WestBow Press
A Division of Thomas Nelson & Zondervan
1663 Liberty Drive
Bloomington, IN 47403
www.westbowpress.com
1 (866) 928-1240

ISBN: 978-1-4908-3528-0 (sc)
ISBN: 978-1-4908-3530-3 (hc)
ISBN: 978-1-4908-3529-7 (e)

Library of Congress Control Number: 2014907582

Print information available on the last page.

WestBow Press rev. date: 5/1/2014

Contents

Acknowledgments

To the Master of all, by whom all things exist: God, thank you for giving us life, that we may experience what it felt like when you produced us, your prize creation. Anything good that comes out of us has come down from the Father of lights. Therefore, we take no credit for what we produce, but we praise you for the life and opportunity to serve you in our endeavor to serve your purpose.

If I were to mention everyone who influenced my life from childhood until now, the chronicle would have to bear pages under its own cover. There are so many people that I leaned on and learned from during the stages of my short lifetime, but time and limitations do not afford me the opportunity to stage every plot. In my life, I am fortunate to have had mentors who became father and mother, friends who became sister and brother, parents who became friends, and siblings who remained close companions. All gave me memories and influence that never left me, even after a long time has passed, and all have gone their separate ways down their own paths.

To my birth parents, the late evangelist and pastor Eugene Stokes Sr. and my ever-loving mother, who will be around for time to come. Thank you, Mama. The many blessings that a real mother contributes cannot be compensated by merely writing pages in a book. However, the advice and instructions that seemed so harsh at times turned out to be as wholesome as your hearty, home-cooked meals and the warmth of your motherly hands in the middle of the night, rubbing down and medicating your eleven kids with home remedies when we were sick. If I were to write a book about you, it would be called *The Voice That Was Louder Than Jesus*. What I thought was fussing turned out to be Jesus' instructions, spoken aloud through the mouth of a loving mother.

I understand now that the arm of discipline broken from the limb of a tree was the hand of the Lord that I needed so that life would not break me. The whippings you gave, along with those long, loud talks, spoke louder than the trouble I would have walked into when you were not around. It was the Lord's advice, spoken with your voice, and what I heard kept me out of grave trouble. I guess what I want to say now that I couldn't say then is "Thank you, Mama, for the switch." It was the switch that turned on the consciousness of righteousness when I was alone and wanted to do wrong. I understand now after I stepped out into this big world that I thought I understood that love hurts. But it is also healthy. Thank you.

To Apostle John Ervin: Standing next to you, I have felt what it must have been like for Peter to walk with Jesus. The admiration, respect, and love I have for you can't be expressed in the pages of a book. My mentor, father, brother, and friend: thank you for handling me with such kindness and tenderness, for telling me without blinking an eye that something good was going to happen. The sacrifice that you and your family made to bring the gospel of the Word to a southern community may have been forgotten by many, but what may have meant nothing to others is of great price in the eyes of the Master, and to me it is priceless love. Thanks for letting me be your son.

To Josh, my brother, my confidant, and my friend: You are a blessing. I can't remember one single time when you were not there as a preacher, an uncompromising confidant that gave balance to my decision making. Your strength and encouragement, with boldness and faith from God, strengthen others. I feel safe and confident when I am around such a strong preacher of faith. Know where your strength lies.

To Ms. Ora Holloway, the sweet, gentle, uncompromising prophetess and precious author, who knows not her own strength: Special thanks to you for blessing my soul with your kind words and encouragement, and for your expertise and guidance in writing this book. I love you much and will see you soon.

To Dr. Eugene Stokes Jr., my brother and friend: It is a privilege to have access to such diversity of knowledge and to receive such sound wisdom without having to make an appointment. The kingdom of heaven suffereth violence, and the radical takes it by force. The family is blessed to have you. Dr. Stokes and Prophetess Jewell, take the state. The city can't handle all that you are offering.

To Ollie, Minnie, William Earl, my precious Carrie, Archie, and James Inett: We will forever be knitted together. We have a job to do, and the time is ripe. I love you. God bless you.

I offer special thanks to the people who were friends for only a short time before we connected as family. Thanks for everything. To Mr. Purnell Hogan: Man! Whenever the phrase "a friend who sticks closer than a brother" comes to mind, you are at the top of my list. I can't thank you enough for everything! Whoever said that blood is thicker than water didn't have Mr. Hogan as a friend. I love you, and God bless. To Mrs. Cathy Williamson (Stokes), a charming, beautiful, intellectual genius in your own right: Distance and time cannot not keep us apart forever. I love you still. To Mr. and Mrs. Brian Sullivan: You are so precious to me. Never forget it. To Mrs. Lucretia Gordon and to Mrs. Brenda, our mutual friend with whom we served in a war zone: Thank you both for good inspiration and for powerful, godly conversation that created a peaceful atmosphere in the midst a hostile environment. To Pastor C. Porter and his wife, of Kingdom Connection: thanks for everything, truly. To Pastor Hazel Taylor, an awesome woman who stays in the face of God: continue in excellence. To the Timmons Holy Temple family and the Vanardo family: I love and miss you all. Thank you so very, very much for your TLC and kindness beyond what should have been shown to a stranger. To Ms. Jerlene Cooper and Ms. Viola Jurden: There is something about you two beautiful ladies. I don't know whether to call you Mama, or Sister, but I do know that you are true friends. I love you and thank you for making me feel special whenever I am in your presence.

To SSG Fredrick Lamar Watson: I love you, my brother. To my brother, SFC Keith Gerald: If I even start to thank you, I will have to write a book. All I will say now is that I love you more than words can express, but you'd better still be singing it right: "I'm coming, Lord." To SSG Michael Byrd, SSG Patrick Tate, 1SG Fonseca, SSG Quichocho, and Colonel Kulp: you are the epitome of leadership. To my brothers in arms: Thank you for the beautiful times we shared in both peace and war. May God continue to keep you until we have a reunion. God bless.

To those who are far better off now than when they were here, but who have left their love, laughs, and the memories of their unique characters as a priceless inheritance that influenced my life: I didn't get a chance to say all that I could have or wanted to say before you left. Thank you for your lives and for affording me the opportunity to learn from you and lean on you.

To the greatest father and one of the greatest among preachers, the late evangelist Eugene Stokes Sr.: Daddy, thank you for being a father and for obeying the voice of God when he called. I remember vividly your laughs and sense of humor that made others laugh. Your message "Launch Out into the Deep" was one of the most profound messages ever preached.

Thank you for providing a roof over my head, clothes to wear, and food to eat. Above all, thank you for leading your family in the path of Jesus.

To Elder A. G. and Mrs. Green: thank you for coming to the backwoods of a cotton field to minister to the Stokes family. To precious Mother Timmons: thank you for giving me opportunities to spread my wings while still learning how to walk. To Mr. Charlie Hunter Jr., brother and young man of valor: I'm sorry you left so soon, but in that short time, you gave a lot. To Mrs. Princella "Mama" Vanardo: thank you for letting me be your son and grow with your family. To Mrs. Angel Vanardo, percussionist, psalmist, and sister: It's been a pleasure being your friend. Thanks for the conversations that always ended in laughter. All of you were truly a gift. Each of you uniquely influenced my life with your presence.

To all of my brothers in arms, who rendered selfless service with valor and paid the ultimate price fighting this country's battles: From one combat soldier to another, I salute you. You are not forgotten.

Last, but certainly not least, exceptional thanks goes to my immediate family, who allotted me the time and space to do the will of God. I love you, and there is more to come.

PART I
THE OTHER WOMAN

For she hath cast down many wounded; yes,
strong men have been slain by her;
her house is the way to hell, going down
to the chambers of death.

Proverbs 7:26–27 (KJV)

MS. FORTUNE

There she sat to the right side of the back door, on the steps of the doctor's office that faced the front entrance of a dead-end street bitterly weeping and afraid. Except for an empty bag that hung from her arm by one of its two straps, she was alone. Her feet were moistened by the tears that fell in a steady drip from between the seams of her palms, pressed desperately against her face. She struggled with the reality of old news, which was also bad news. "Lord, why are you picking on me?" she vented.

Other than the doctor, only the banker understood the seriousness of her problem. Her bank statement and body language made the same sad statement: both was exhausted but still bleeding out. Outraged with her God, infuriated by her doctor, and frustrated with herself, she proclaimed, "This is my last trip!" After slapping both hands on her knees, she shouted, "Is this a doctor's office, or what? I feel more like a criminal than a patient. One hundred visits, but still one verdict!" She angrily rambled on. "For five years I've been running to and from this office. After all the appointments I have kept, this place still feels like a courtroom, because, like a judge, the doctor keeps sentencing me to death!"

Wailing through the denial phase of the metamorphic stage of acceptance, the rage continued. "If you are my judge, Lord, what is my crime? Time after time I've prayed, but my prayers are just as empty as my purse, and like my purse, there is no change in my body. These prayers to you have been a waste of time, and these visits to the doctor are a waste of my money. If the doctor can't stop the bleeding, what's the use in coming?"

She was giving up on the doctor, and herself as well. Being sick, with no strength left to stand and fight, she sighed into a moment of silence before rising slowly from the steps. After the name-calling and recognizing that she had no one else to blame, she finally had no more tears to cry. Her mourning subsided in the quietness of her own mind, as she made plans for her short future.

She concluded, "God, I'm not a bad person. I don't bother anyone. I love my neighbors, just as you command. I have paid taxes to the man, but you have paid no attention to me, even though I have kept your laws and have even paid a tenth to the priest. Although I am angry, I am not a fool that I should curse God and die. But sometimes I feel, in my faintest and most trying hour, that I should. If you don't help me, Lord and you have a choice then I haven't a chance, because the doc doesn't have a clue.

"Although I cry, there is one thing I simply refuse to do: pay another visit or penny to one other doctor to hear him preach my funeral. Since it seems that I am destined to taste death, I owe it to myself to take matters into my own hands. Instead of going to the marketplace to spend the only money I have left on food, I will take my chances with the undertaker, where I know my money will do me some good."

When the substances that give life to your world begin bleeding out, the world you live in can become frustrating. One uncontrollable circumstance in this woman's life triggered another life-draining issue. Her issue of blood created an issue at the bank. Lack of change in her body demanded the change in her purse. Her whole life's savings had gone down the drain, because her body wouldn't stop bleeding.

But that's the kind of world we've inherited from our first father. Adam failed. When he dropped the ball, he also dropped a bomb, leaving us with all kinds of holes that we could fall into. One man's disobedience introduced this world to a host of uncontrollable, life-changing issues:

At this moment, someone just walked out of the doctor's office with a clean bill of health, only to walk into his or her own house to meet a table piled with bills, like the mound of a grave. Your health may be on top of the mountain, but unfortunately you are drowning in debt. Although you are physically healthy, you are buried financially. You have a clean bill of health but no money to pay the bills. Isn't it funny? A single circumstance beyond this woman's control resulted in a financial abyss.

This whole planet was supposed to have been a vineyard, springing forth with health, wealth, wellness, harmony, peace, love, and wholeness. Instead, it has become a graveyard, just the opposite of what God intended to grow out of the earth. Leech like issues can bleed you into a hole. Instead of health, there is sickness; instead of wealth, poverty; instead of wellness, weariness; instead of harmony, havoc; instead of peace, destruction; instead of love, hate; instead of wholeness, holes everywhere! If we're not climbing out of one ditch, we're falling into a deeper hole.

Every now and then, everyone would like to get away from life's bitterness and enjoy more pleasant scenery. The grade-A diagnosis from your doctor affords you the ability to participate in any activity you like. You can go anywhere in the world you desire, and stay in the finest of suites as long as you like. So, there you stand on a balcony of a luxurious high-rise, only a few feet from the shores of a white, sandy beach, enjoying the scenery of sky-blue water and the soothing sounds of waves tugged back and forth by the sweet summer breeze. With this amazing view, no candles are required, as you dine on the terrace of your plush suite with a full, glowing moon surrounded by constellations. How fortunate you are to be in picture-perfect health, which allows you to enjoy such wonders as you sail the seven seas, getting a small taste of life outside the everyday routines you have known your whole life. Unfortunately for you, this sweet vacation ends with the bitter voice of your alarm clock awakening you to the reality of your poor financial status, reminding you that your dream vacation is but a dream that always ends in a waking nightmare.

Some people are fortunate to be heirs to family fortunes, where they stand to inherit billions. In their lifetimes, these heirs and heiresses will never know poverty, financial strain, or lack. And some of these will inherit an illness or disease from the same family members who worked their fingers to the bone so that their heirs would never would have to lift a finger to be financially stable. The heirs may be worth billions, but inherited physical misfortunes only afford them a million-to-one chance of ever enjoying a healthy lifestyle. Financial wealth afford these heirs access to the the top floor of some of the world's finest hotels, and it frees them to swim on some of the most exotic beaches. Unfortunately, poor health will not allow them to lift a finger to help themselves or to walk into the next room to shower their own bodies.

These heirs can afford to eat the most exotic foods, yet how unfortunate that poor health confines them to a five-by-seven room in an intensive care unit that reduces them from eating solid foods from a silver spoon to feeding on liquids from a plastic tube. Billion-dollar heirs with access to private jets are grounded, because the misfortune of impoverished health is somewhere in the wind.

As in the life of the woman with the issue of blood, one bleeding issue can easily breed another life-draining trauma. One issue can bring drama to our whole life. If we want to live, that life-draining issue becomes our priority, leaving us without much life outside of our issue. All kinds of issues roam about our lives, bleeding the very life out of living.

Some people have landed in a hole of depression, because they have lost their jobs and families over what was meant to be a quick, casual, friendly drink while celebrating with a colleague. Now, they spend most of their lives in a ten-by-ten-foot chamber, meeting with other unfortunate souls who are struggling to climb out of the same hole. Everyone hopscotches through life's journey, dodging holes. Right now, some spouses bleat in the night, because they are trapped in the web of an abusive marriage that's beating the daylights out of them.

You could be suffocating inside the glass of a crack pipe because you tried to escape the problems of this life only to discover that life outside the glass is not the worst life to live. Every unfortunate mishap that ever has happened or will happen, now exists because the axle of the world slipped away from the original intent of God's plan, including the bodily functions of man.

An unbalanced metabolism may have cast you into an abyss of obesity. Some people, even though they are not addicts, because of an imbalance in blood sugar are demanded to use the needle. Whether you have unbalanced blood sugar or high blood pressure, you end up in figurative handcuffs and spend "ten to twenty" in a five-by-seven-foot "cell" because of peer pressure. Either way, through an unfortunate situation, an unbalanced world has brought you face-to-face with Ms. Fortune.

But don't you worry. The last atomic "balm" dropped from heaven onto the earth came to soothe our hurts, seal up our wounds, and open up our graves, pulling us out of the many holes created by the first Adam's bomb. You are not in a place where the Master doesn't travel. In Jesus' day, anyone who looked for him found him among people who were just like us downtrodden, beaten up, strung out, mistreated, misused, misunderstood, and getting dressed for the next funeral. That's the reason he came. Jesus always walked among the dead, pulling men out fetters and chains. He roamed among the sick and the wounded. They could always find him in the gutter or the ghetto.

Be careful, though. Ms. Fortune does not discriminate in distributing mishap and havoc. Mayhem and mortuaries are found in the palaces of kings as well as the potter's field. They search for the sons of presidents and the daughters of paupers, the prestigious and the poor, the well-off and the no-good. Despite how careful we are, whether we have worked hard to conquer kingdoms or have accomplished nothing, no one can avoid looking into the eyes of Ms. Fortune. Whether our misfortune is involuntary (through inheritance or accident) or voluntary (because we thought we could control it), happenstance (random) or purposeful (because we took a chance and made it happen), expected or unexpected, we all, sooner or later, will come face-to-face with Ms. Fortune, because in the beginning, Adam lost control of the garden.

Make no mistake about what or whom the Master was looking for when he came. Indeed, he was looking for both Ms. Fortune and Ms. Carry. It is documented that anywhere he found Ms. Fortune, misbehaving and looking to miscarry a situation, the Master always caused Ms. Carry to misfire. When someone was trapped, mistreated, starving, sick, or disabled, and the situation was grave, he came onto the scene.

It has yet to be seen where the righteous were forsaken.

If you have no bread, say not that life is over and done. There is no need to beg, for it has been written that the sick are delivered out of their beds with only his crumbs and some by only a thread.

What's going on out there? she wondered.

Just as she was finalizing the arrangements for her burial with her last piece of change, a distraction echoed from a town meeting on the village square and drew her attention away from her transaction with the mortician. Before she could finish her thought, the name *Jesus* again echoed through the town. The woman walked slowly to the window for a quick peek, only to see a crowd larger than she had perceived.

Master! The calling grew louder, as the crowd grew broader in the square. Finally, curiosity shoved her clean out the door of the funeral parlor and into the streets with the nasty, pressing crowd. *Healer!* Whether the cry came from the crowd, from around the corner, or from within herself, she could not tell. She didn't care. While others continued crying out to the man in the middle of the square, she was already on hands and knees, crawling through the masses toward the man in the center of town.

Suddenly, the congregation grew quiet and still, for they heard a cry from the one who was the center of their attention. "Who touched me?" shouted the Master. Bewildered by Jesus' question, the disciples looked around. Curious about who had touched him, the Master looked around as well. Seeing that Jesus was surrounded by so many people, the crowd was as confused as the disciples. They quickly looked to each other for an explanation for such a stupid question.

As the Master searched for the answer to his question, he looked down to find that his garment had come undone at the hem. Slowly, the people parted like the red sea as he traced the unravaling thread of his garment into the middle of the pressing crowd. The people didn't know exactly what he was doing, but that was okay, because he was the Master. All eyes gazed upon him as he patiently walked forward.

A few steps farther into the press at the other end of the thread unraveled from his garment, like a fish on a line he found a woman on her knees. All were amazed and staring steadfastly at the him, but with her eyes fastened shut, and a hymn in her heart she had put on the garment of praise. Her head was bowed down, her hands were raised. She was unraveling glory from heaven worshipping God for the deed done in her body, and for saving her from the grave.

The good woman bowed down in the center of town would not have known that she was now center of attention in the middle of the crowd, except for the shadow cast by the Son. The message in her tears that ran down each cheek to meet at the bottom of her face was not clear. Was she afraid that she had done something unacceptable, or was she simply over whelm by the healing that had taken place in her body? Concluding in her own mind that she would face her fears. *For whatever punishment for receiving this healing,* she thought, *no dungeon could be worse than the ditch jesus has just brought me out of.* More overjoyed than afraid she opened her eyes.

Much to her surprise, there hovered the shadow of love with dove-soft eyes. The Son shone down upon her face with a gentle smile filled with grace, staring right back into her crying eyes that embraced her grateful, humbled soul. Silently, with a touch as soft as cotton, he held her damp hand that had been moistened by her tears in his palm coercing her to be lifted up. Suddenly she realized, in spite of what she had done, that He was not a monster, but a master. The kind that pick servants up, and bring them out instead of putting people down and doing them in. In a moment of reverence, the woman resisted standing. Thanking him in any position other than bowing would not be just, she thought.

As his feet and her head touched, she sobbed. "Master,

I'm sorry about the hem," she said. After kneeling to kiss his feet, she leaned back on her heels and looked up at him through the veil of the waterfall that ran down her face. She whispered, "But, Lord, thank you for the thread." The Master's tears anointed her head, and she knew not why he wept. But he was overjoyed that her health was no longer in a rut. Only after she'd left the place where they had met did she realize that Jesus had known, as she did, that whereas the hem of his gown had fallen down, her wound had been stitched up.

He that is made whole needs not a physician, but he that is ensnared in a hole should expect a visit from the Master. Unfortunately, the disobedience of the first Adam left us open to being snared by the nets of a worldwide web of predators: Ms. Fortune, Ms. Treated, Ms. Carry, and Ms. Used." When we escape the tragedy of being brought down into the pit of one, two more are waiting around the next corner, with other issues that can get us all hemmed up. All types of problems are everywhere, because of one man's disobedience.

But thank God for the answer that came to deliver us out of them all. He has more in his hem to seal up our bleeding wounds and mend our broken hearts. He says that he has come to preach the gospel to the poor, to open blinded eyes and prison doors, and to bring prisoners out of the dark that they may see the Son. Anywhere Ms. Fortune and Ms. Carry are found, Jesus rescues those who are abused, mistreated, or misused, and his mission hasn't changed.

MS. 2 USED

One day while walking about and doing the Father's business, the Master ran into a few businessmen who were not necessarily in the cleaning business preparing to toss out the town's dirty laundry. Well within their lawful rights, they were sure that the Master would applaud their efforts.

"Master, the law says that if one among us should be found in adultery, she should be stoned," the ringleader boldly rattled off. "What say you?"

Sitting at the village well as if he hadn't heard a word, the Master did not respond. He continued pouring water from a small vase onto his dusty feet. Just when the bold speaker, who thought he was being ignored, opened his mouth to repeat his words, the Master calmly and respectfully replied to the witnesses with a question. "Which of you is the harlot?"

Appalled by the Master's question, the witness said, "What do you mean, which of us is the harlot?" One of the brutal lawmen, who had seemingly already passed judgment in this case, was holding the poor girl by the tender back part of her neck. "Isn't it obvious?"

"Well," said the Master, "seeing that you want me to be a judge of this matter, there are thirteen of you."

Another of the twelve jurors at the back of the small posse of witnesses shouted, "Thirteen? Are you blind? There is only one woman here! Are you even a master?"

Gently Jesus replied, "I'm not, and I am."

"Well, do something about this!"

"I cannot," said the Lord.

"So you don't know the law, then?" the angry accuser yelled. "If you cannot judge such a simple matter as this, how can you call yourself a master?"

"Sir," the Master said to the plaintiff, "it is against the law to mislead witnesses, and lest I misjudge this matter falsely, my judgment at the moment is for the accused, because the scale is unbalanced."

"Well!" shouted the young fellow, ignoring Jesus' statement and anxiously and angrily awaiting a response he could understand. When there was no immediate reply from the Master, he continued. "Enough of this gibberish. Since you don't know the law, we will continue our business here." All the plaintiffs agreed, and the jurors stepped away to fulfill the law.

The Master answered in love. "The accused indeed deserves death according to the letter of the law, because the letter kills, but I have come that you may have life. So, my friend, before we put this woman into the grave that you have dug for her, bring me the men that kept her in business." The witnesses' twelve mouths and twenty-four bricks dropped to the ground. "Furthermore," Jesus went on, "all you who have no dirt of your own, throw the first brick."

Three seconds later, Jesus asked the woman, "Where are your accusers?"

"Lord," the woman replied, "my best customers just slithered away."

If you had been living at the time when Jesus, the Word of Life, physically walked the earth, you would have often found him in the midst of such grave situations, freeing those who were obviously guilty and were caught in a snare. If you are in a dirty business or have done something dirty, Jesus does not seek to throw you away like trash, because he does not take you at face value. It benefits his Father's business to brush off the dirt, take you to the cleaners, wash you in his blood, baptize you with his water, and make you clean, because he knows there is something awesome deep inside you.

"For you are clean through the Word I have spoken unto you." No one can tell you how long your appointed grace period is. Even so, we don't want to make a habit of taking unnecessary risks with his mercy, once it has been delivered. Our God of mercy has a change of garments for us. The judge's robe is just a hand's length away. Therefore, son or daughter, do what Jesus said: "Go and sin no more."

It is not my business how you got into your mess. It is the Father's business, and his mission for Jesus was and is to bring you out of your hole. He was the backup, who came down to fix up and to build up from the grave what the first Adam had messed up, mixed up, and torn up. That's why the plan of salvation demanded that the Tree of Life be planted among graves, and what the Master has done cannot be undone.

Ms. Phitts

After the fall of Adam, God regretted that he had ever made man, but he had too much invested to destroy the whole planet because of one man's disobedience. So God simply began again.

To God, it was nothing strange to look within the earth to find a cemetery to restart the life he had first begun. Before the beginning of the world, he had stepped out onto nothingness. While browsing through near-oblivion, he saw it: spaced out in her own world of water and mist, it waited on nothing. It was unproductive and without shape, invalid, unresponsive, and void (dead). It wanted nothing, and nothing wanted it. It was dead weight, hanging there without structure. Not that it didn't have a form, because the fact that a thing exists means that it has some type of shape. But this thing in that place, before he moved upon it, was not in any shape to produce.

People, places, and things that have no structure for production may seem to us like dead weight and a waste of time, but they are an opportunity for God to lift a burden, raise the dead and makes a worthless thing worthwhile. So it's ok if, at times you feel like a misfit. God didn't misplace you he knows exactly who you are. He knew where he place you when he fitted you into his plan. You are not a mistake. Even before there was a beginning, God brought forth life out of something that was void and fit for nothing. So it was not strange that God when he looked within the earth after Adam had introduced us to death would go into another graveyard to bring forth life.

THE DIVINE PLAN

In God's own timing, he sketched the plan of salvation and stretched it out upon the plain of time. The blueprint of redemption would unfold throughout the course of several generations before it would be completed.

To begin his plan, God found a dead tree, from whose loins he would bring the Tree of Life. Within God's divine plan, he waited until Abram was well-stricken in years. But even if God had called out to Abram before the effects of erectile dysfunction set in, the prospect of producing a son during his productive years would still have encountered a problem.

Abram was like a dead tree from whom the Tree of Life was to spring. Still in his green years, the seed was alive in his loins, but the malfunction was found in her with whom he was planted. Sarai was a pleasant woman to look upon, in that she had landed Abram, and she was a good woman as well as a good person. Sarai, even in her childbearing years, could not conceive seed to yield fruit unto Abram. Simply put, Abram was a doubly dead treedead once because he didn't know the true and living God before God approached him, and dead again, though he had a living physical body, because he could no longer could produce a child of his own loins, and he was married to a tomb.

If a dead tree and a tomb do not constitute a grave situation, nothing does. When God stepped into the deadness of Abram and Sarai's life to do a work in that graveyard, neither Abram nor his wife was physically fit for the purpose of his visit, nor did they understand the significance of his approach. God never visits without map in hand or a plan in mind. He moves upon a person, place, or thing to do one out of three or all three impossible things: to pull you out of something that you, by your own strength, cannot get loose from; to pull something out of you that cannot be revealed except he moves upon you; or to pull out of you something that *you* desire to be loosed.

The water and mist that hung in the balance of the world were capable of producing their own kind: the ocean, seas, waterfalls, rivers, and streams. But how was something dry to come out of something wet? The water was unfit to bring forth dry land, but the hand of the Lord moved upon the face of the deep to do a work in her depths, because God did not take the water at face value.

As soon as the hand of the Lord moved upon the face of the waters and pulled out the earth, God demanded that the earth bring forth from her dry land and streams an abundance of fruit. That would have been just fine, if God had demanded only a glass of water from her rivers and a handful of berries or a bushel of apples from the trees, branches, and vines she was designed to produce. But where on the earth did flesh and bones grow? From what creek could be drawn fresh blood to bring forth Adam?

Because the earth was not fit by design to bring forth men, she had to wait for the crafty hand of the Lord to moved upon her. This was one move she could not make without him just as men were not made to bring forth women, but God used what he had and moved upon the male to bring forth Eve. Whenever the hand of the Lord moves upon a person, place, or thing, he causes it to produce something that it can't ordinarily produce on its own.

For this cause, at the beginning of the divine plan of

salvation, the hand of God made a move on Sarai. Whenever the body of a woman, for whatever reason, malfunctions and cannot manufacture babies as it was designed to do, then the womb, made to be an incubator for holding live bodies, takes on the nature of a tomb. Unless God does something, there is no way a live body will come out of a grave, because a tomb, like a barren woman, is incapable of releasing live bodies.

When we consider the similarities and differences, we note that the tomb is an incubator with walls that preserve bodies. The womb has the necessary surroundings for preserving bodies until it's time for the exodus of the baby. The tomb is a reservoir for the dead and has no expected exit; the womb is reserved for the living and an expected delivery. The tomb is for burying; the womb for birthing. The tomb is a morgue that holds the dead; the womb is a receptacle that mothers the living.

Unfortunately, the tomb is by nature a nonbearing module ... ordinarily. Double-dead Sarai, unable to bear children and well-stricken in age, who did not know the living God before his approach, could not, for the life of her, produce live bodies. Needless to say, Sarai was not physically fit to have babies, which caused God to move upon her. Fortunately for Sarai and for us, when God visits a person or moves upon a place, it is to pull something out of the deep, rather than to take the grave at face value. When God steps into a grave situation and moves upon a tomb, regardless of the form in which it presents itself, something comes out of it.

THE REHEARSAL AND THE REALITY

While Pilate washed his hands of the Savior's innocence, the finale of the plan of salvation burst out of the courtroom, into the courtyard, and along the path to Calvary with our own death penalty hanging over Jesus' head. Beneath the thorns set so harshly upon his brow, the gentle crown of wisdom revealed all the images that God had planted in his mind on his way to the grave, so that Jesus, during his horrific trial, might maintain strength to endure by remembering the outcome of his suffering. Soldiers hewed branches from an entangled bush of thorns and crammed them around jesus' head. Even if the arms o the Lamb hadn't been tied to the sacricicial stake, he would not have bothered to remove them, because he understood why his head was caught in the bush.

The rehearsal for Jesus' sacrifice involved the horn of a ram, the head of a lamb, and the form of a man. In that rehearsal, the lad Isaac inquired of his father, Abraham, about the lamb to be sacrificed. Abraham told him not to worry about it, that God would provide.

In reality, Emmanuel didn't bother asking this question of almighty God, his Father. Without mumbling a word, the Lamb kept quiet. He knew that he was the real provision. Our Lord understood the layout of the plan of salvation that had begun with Father Abraham. It had been designed so that all images, shadows, and figures of the rehearsal would feature an all-star cast in the finale.

Abram the dead tree who could not, before he met God, produce a child from his loins and Sarai the tomb who had never borne life from her womb were actual persons in the rehearsal. And the cast from the rehearsal were revealed upon the stage of the actual event at Calvary.

In spite of the Savior's pain, he had to remain on the stake. He had to fill the space in that awful place and be burned in the fire in our stead and for our sake just as a ram caught in a bush was burned on the sticks as a sacrifice in place of Abraham's son, Isaac. Jesus, Alpha and Omega, was stained and hung on the cross to bear the sin of the world so that we, like Isaac, could escape the flames. Afterward, he would overcome the sting of death that we involuntarily inherited through the disobedience of our father Adam. Our Savior had not sinned, nor was guile found in his mouth, but he was made sin for us.

He had not the strength to raise his head, he somehow managed to pull his thorn-crowned head away from the cross. As though the arm of the Roman empire by the whip of the soldiers had not done enough, he struggled to keep his head steady with the little life left in him. The hand of gravity sided suddenly with the power of the enemy and bore down upon his wobbling, weak head, burying his chin upon his now sunken chest between his limp, slumped shoulders. Waltzing from side to side, his eyes, for loss of blood, danced up and down. In his tender, frail state, he failed to remain conscious. After all the beatings, Christ had taken his last breath.

After an hour without movement from any part of his body, much of the crowd was convinced that death had closed the door on the final chapter, and they turned to walk away from the cross. Then, lo and behold, much to their surprise, Jesus managed to birth through his swollen lips the whisper of a single word: "Woman." Then he sighed and went back into a mute state of unconsciousness.

The poorly pronounced word and the fainting murmur uttered by the Word of Life was not enough entertainment to further the stay of unbelieving onlookers. This left only a faithful few to witness, fifteen minutes later, a dim ray of life from the Master. He stared through a dead man's stupor, peeking from beneath the eyelids of the one engorged eye that could still open, and looked down in the only direction he could. He saw, kneeling powerless in a puddle of his blood mingled with her tears, his mother.

Through the blurry waterfall that poured down her face, she mournfully looked up. Desperately awaiting the Master's words, she intercepted a murmur from the lips of a decrepit Savior. Finishing the phrase he had first begun to mutter,

Jesus said to her, "Behold thy son." It was a personal and final farewell from her Lord and Master, but mostly from her son.

Then she and the men standing with her deciphered from the stammering lips of their dying son and friend: "Son, behold thy mother." It was a final order from their Master and Lord for them to take care of Mary. In response to their defeated Master's final request, the disciples who often heard his words but seldom understood what he meant turned to the mother who had borne him and gently escorted Mary away from the horrific scene of the shame and into the pavilion of their own homes.

However good their intentions were, their ignorance of what he had just done was no different from all the misconception they had conceived before the cross. Immediately, in their carnality, though out of compassion, the disciples took hold of Mary, the mother who was standing beside them. There are more reasons to believe that our Master's command, "Woman, behold thy son," was directed instead, or as much to the earth, the "mother" they were standing on, as it was to Mary. The command made by the Master was not so much a farewell to the former surrogate as it was an introduction to a cemetery, the one that was about to be artificially inseminated by the Word of Life.

Be not dismayed because I say that he called this tomb "Woman." The Master's love, known to his men, should have provoked a question in at least one of the twelve: "Why would a man one who so loved the world that he would lay down his life for his friends ask the woman who had given him life to gaze upon such a horrific sight of her son?"

Similarly, the woman Sarai was just as incapable of bringing forth Isaac, as the cemetery was of producing Emmanuel. One grave is just as void as another, even if the grave is the body of a woman. You understand that the tomb was no more a woman than the woman Sarai was a tomb, but

God required that a body come out of the grave, just as he was calling for a body to come out of Sarai. Although Sarai was a woman, she, like the grave, could not produce a man. When it came to either the womb of Sarai or the tomb at Calvary yielding up a body, both were dead. Both were unfit for the task.

If changing Sarai's name had caused a body to come out of her, though she was just as dead as a grave when it came to producing a body, then the grave, which was not even human, needed a name change as well. Therefore, the Master looking down at both mothers but directing his attention to her who had not yet borne him and could not yet do so called her by the only name that produces men. To one it was a farewell, and to the other it was an introduction. Twenty-one years earlier, the Master had already told his first surrogate that he had to be about his Father's business. Although Mary had divinely conceived without the seed of a man, her divine business with the Savior ended in Bethlehem at the manger. However, his divine business with the grave began on the cross at Calvary.

If changing a name, such as God did to Sarai, could cause a dead thing to produce after the name it was called, then it was the grave, more than Mary, who needed to be called "Woman." In spite of hanging on a cross, Jesus was still on the divine clock, and part of the divine process, according to protocol, meant giving the dead tomb a name in keeping with what he needed the tomb to produce just as Sarai, during the "rehearsal," was called on to produce after the name Sarah. Nothing came out of Sarai until she was renamed Sarah.

Jesus made the call before he entered the tomb, so that when he was planted, the thing he'd spoken to would produce after the name by which he had called her. Therefore, the Master called the cemetery by the only name that manufactures men, so that the ground he was about to enter would, in three days, divinely perform according to a name she had been called, rather than according to the nonbearing module that she was.

If there is anything you know that needs another name because it is not producing after the name it is presently called, then you have the power to call it by another name.

Jesus' heart was beating slowly from a loss of blood, which was dripping as fast as the divine clock, but he was still required to finish his divine business with the grave. In spite of hanging on by a thread, Emmanuel's divine business would not be done until he had come out of his grave, just as Sarah's business was not finished until Isaac exited the dead body of Sarai. His pressing business and priority at Calvary, as well as his last breath, were directed toward the next surrogate that was about to be artificially inseminated with the Word of Life.

Mary had done an awesome job of bringing Jesus into this world, and it was fine that she was there, but she had already produced by divine intervention. Even if a man could enter the second time into the womb of his mother and be born again, Jesus was still obligated by divine appointment to be borne again directly out of the cradle of the ground.

Jesus understood that when he said, "Woman"and his disciples innocently beheld Mary instead of beholding the cemetery they had once again misunderstood what he was doing. The last Adam had come as a pattern of the first, and although Alpha was the Lord from above who had come through the birth canal of a woman, Omega's next birth would be a C-section performed on the grave. The Son of Man had to be extracted directly from the belly of Mother Earth by the hand of God, just as Adam, the first fleshly male, had been extracted from the cradle of the ground.

On both occasions concerning Sarai and the graveGod was calling for a body. In either case, both "women" were unfit for the task. When the Word at Calvary said, "Woman," his message was evidently directed to the tomb, because the cemetery responded to the call. Calling the grave *woman* was no more than the angel Gabriel calling a virgin *mother*. After Jesus' salutation and command, the tomb did what Mary had done thirty-three years earlier. Since the divine occasion at Calvary demanded that a man must come out of a tomb, it was appropriate that a cemetery like Sarai, who was called by another name so that she would produce kings be called by a name that would bring forth men.

THE ADAM SAGA

Only the first Adam came directly out of the earth. Every man thereafter came out of the woman. In the beginning, God used the earth to produce the first man, because only he is self-existent. Everything else has a beginning. Therefore, all things begin with him. God did not create an apparatus to manufacture men. It pleased him that everything produced after its own kind, and he would not have used the ground in the beginning if there had been a woman to lend her womb, but Eve had not yet been born out of the bone of Adam.

What else was God to do? He was ready to begin the life of mankind, but he wanted the male to be the first human creature. So he moved upon the earth and substituted the earth for the body of a woman by covering the whole earth in water, using the submerged earth as an egg and the sea that covered the earth as the water sac of a woman. To compensate for the absence of a womb, he formed the body of the first man from a submerged earth, thus creating the pattern after which every man would be born of a woman (Genesis 2:5–7). After Eve was brought forth and demonstrated the means by which man would be conceived and produced, the earth was relieved of her duty to ever produce another man. Thereafter, God used the woman to bring forth men on the earth, including the last Adam.

But it was not enough for the Son of Man to come out of a woman. If Jesus, the last Adam, was to fit the birth patterns of the first Adam and demonstrate that God had truly begun again and restored mankind's access to the sinless life of the first Adam then he had to be divinely extracted directly from the cradle of the grave, just as the first Adam had been divinely extracted from the ground. To meet the qualifications of the "Adam saga," the last Adam had to be born of a woman, and then be born again directly from the dust, because the first Adam did not come from a woman. Somehow, Jesus had to be brought alive out of the belly of the earth even if he had to go to the grave to meet the qualification because the first Adam, when he came out of the dirt of the earth, was a living soul (1 Corinthians 15:45).

This divine process would also distinguish Jesus from false messiahs. None could proclaim to be saviors if they got stuck in death the very thing they were to save mankind from. Only a Messiah who is resurrected can save man from the grave.

Another qualification for meeting the requirements of being an "Adam" figure presents a problem as well. The last Adam would be born of a woman, because, after Eve, a woman existed to lend a womb. In the beginning, to begin the life of men, the body of the first man was formed in the belly of the earth by the hand of the Lord, having nothing to do with the seed of a man. Therefore, the body formed within Mary could have nothing to do with Joseph. It must be divinely formed in the belly of Mary by the hand of the Lord.

Therefore, the Father prepared a womb so that the last Adam, although born of a woman, would come out of Mary having a body formed by the hands of the Lord, just as the first Adam had been formed from the earth without the seed of a man (Hebrews 10:5). Because the seed of a man had nothing to do with the existence of the first Adam, it should not be surprising that the last Adam claimed to be the Son of God. If the first Adam, who had no earthly father, had been formed in the belly of the earth and was the son of God (Luke 3:38), then surely Jesus, whose body had been formed by the hand of God in Mary's belly without the seed of a man, should call God his Father. Who, besides God, could have been the father of either one?

You already see the problem, don't you? Even though women have assumed the responsibility of manufacturing men since the first man was delivered out of the belly of the earth, no woman is given the power to conceive without the seed of a man. Therefore, the body of the last Adam had to be formed in the belly of a woman by the same divine means that God used to form the first Adam. What could the God of all existence do, seeing that he required the body of a woman, except move upon Mary not in the manner of a husband with his wife, but in the capacity of a surgeon with his patient? It was not a sexual encounter; it was a divine operation that prepared the body of the last Adam in Mary's body, just as he had formed the body of the first Adam in the belly of the earth.

This divine process used to bring the last Adam to the earth, among a few other things, would also distinguish him from the pretenders who would claim to be the Christ. Any man born of a woman could easily proclaim that he was the Messiah, but how many could claim that they had no earthly father? If you are confused by multiple messiahs, use the process of elimination to find the right Savior. If your messiah has an earthly father, your messiah is not "the last Adam."

God was not intimidated by the grave, because this was not his first time bringing forth a man out of the ground. He did it without the assistance of a human, just as no human had anything to do with the first Adam being extracted from the earth in the beginning. When God did a C-section on the grave to pull the last Adam from the dust of the ground, the dry land at Calvary looked the same as the original dry land from which he had brought forth the first Adam. From the very beginning, God used his Word to bring forth his creation: "And God said ..." So the cross did not intimidate God when the last Adam had to be pulled out of the ground. God's Word caused a thing to perform according to the name by which he called it. In three days, despite wearing the face of a grave, the earth performed like the name Jesus called her: "Woman!"

When the Word of God is spoken into a person, place, or thing, change is inevitable, even if it seems impossible. If God moves upon the face of a thing, he always speaks; and when he speaks, something amazing comes out of its depths, regardless of its outer appearance. Whenever the Word is deposited into anything, expect change, because the Word will never yield a void return on a deposit, even if the situation is grave (Isaiah 55).

Graves don't produce bodies, but neither do the mouths of fish spit out money. When Jesus performed that miracle, the face of the fish stayed the same, but the evidence of change was found in the fish's body. When peter went to the riverbank, change to pay the Master's taxes were found in the mouth of the fish. The face of the bass said "fish," but her body said "ATM" (Matthew 17:27). In the same way, the face of the cemetery said "grave," but on the third day, its body said "woman." Change started taking place, not when Jesus rose from the dead but as soon as he spoke and said, "Woman."

In addition, "Woman, behold thy son" was a statement of faith, and our Lord was a man of faith. He remained faithful unto death, and his faith called to those things that are not, as though they were. While he hung on the tree, the earth lay there as a grave, but what he needed was an apparatus that produced men. Therefore, in faith, he called the grave by the only name ordained to manufacture men: *woman.*

Mary was already a woman, and she had borne other children after the Master's birth. It was the grave that needed to take on the nature of a childbearing woman. Of course, the grave was nothing like Sarai, Mary, or Eve, that it would even be considered to produce a body. But neither was a rock in the desert a pregnant woman. Yet after a particular rock received the word from Moses, her water broke, and a dead, dry rock, of all things, sprang forth with water. Just as the rock was not fit to be a well, neither was the grave fit bring forth bodies. Yet the rock and the grave were the misfits that God chose to use, and after a word from him, they produced.

Henceforth and forever, we who are of faith should no longer be condemned by what's thrown in our faces. Even when all hope is lost and the situation is grave, we should not be intimidated by our circumstances. Instead, we should imitate our Father and speak into the situation to produce what is needed. By appearance, a rock became a well. Which is more insane: to talk to a tomb or to a rock? It was just as insane for Moses to speak to a rock as it was for the Master to salute the grave.

The truth of the matter is, it doesn't matter what something *is* before it is *called*. When the Word of God is spoken into it, it becomes what it has been named, and it will produce out of its depths and perform according to the name it is call, regardless of what the thing it is. When it comes to the Word, "non is barren among them." Anything will produce, if the Word is spoken into it. Not even a dead grave can be barren when it comes to the Word of God (Song of Solomon 6:6).

PUT A KNOT IN IT

Messengers came to the Master and said, "Lazarus, whom thou lovest, is dead." As soon as Jesus heard this, he changed the whole grave situation with one simple phrase: "He is not

35

dead, but sleepeth." Immediately, a knot was lodged in the mouth of the grave so that Lazarus would not be swallowed up by death.

Though every man and everything be liars, what God says is true. A person, place, or thing may put on an impressive face, but once you speak the Word and keep the faith, evidence unseen will materialize in that place. Those who came to the Master were telling the truth; Lazarus was indeed dead. And Lazarus' death was truth to them, because they could not raise him.

Yet they could have raised Lazarus, had they understood the procedures and process of faith. Jesus, understanding faith, went on to Lazarus' location, which everyone was calling a grave. But the Master had said that Lazarus was only sleeping, so the Master went, not to a grave to mourn a dead man, but to a bedroom to awaken a sleeping friend. The moment Jesus said, "He is not dead," unseen changes took place in the depths of the grave. Everything about that "bedroom" outwardly said "morgue," but in the end, Lazarus had to return out of the grave, because he was the refund for the Words deposited by the Master.

Isaiah 55 says that the Word of God is like money. When and where it is deposited, it shall always yield a return. As soon as the doctor says, "You have but six months, and then you're dead," you can lodge a knot in the mouth of cancer so that you will not be swallowed up by the belly of the grave. Whatever hole you're in can't swallow you when a knot from the Word is lodged in its throat: "I shall live and *not* die." Do not say, "Who shall ascend into the heavens to bring Christ back down to the earth to bring me out of whatever grave situation I am facing?" Instead, use a simple phrase to change whatever lie the doctor has told you. Begin as Jesus did by saying, "I shall live and *not* die." In the end, both the doctor and grave will swallow their own words, as soon as they see evidence of the investment you made by your words.

You ought to put a knot into the mouth of whatever is eating away at you. Whatever kind of hole you're in right now will gag on its own message if you believe the words of God that you have spoken into it, regardless of its visible expression. Even though the evidence may not be seen at first, the spoken words of God form a knot in the depths of that thing!

The reality at Calvary was to be a mirror image of Abraham's rehearsal. Had Abraham and Isaac actually been with Jesus at Calvary, they would have understood their role in the rehearsal, and maybe they would not have been so disturbed and distracted about what was going on in their own reality.

Despite the shame, Jesus, the seed of Abraham, remained faithful and peaceful upon the erected tree until he was laid into the ground. The Savior's understanding of the rehearsal was the only comfort he found in being lifted up. In the rehearsal, there could have been no birth from the "tomb" of Sarai until the dead "tree" of Abram was resurrected, and there was no sense in God resurrecting Abraham's tree if Sarai's tomb did not receive strength to bring forth Isaac. While Abraham was being strengthened to plant, Sarai was receiving strength to produce. Therefore, when the *tree* at Calvary was being lifted, it was a sure sign to the Savior that the grave was receiving strength to bring forth life. No seed from any man can be planted, unless there is first a resurrection.

When the soldiers rushed into the courtyard and threw at Jesus' feet the tree that was to be lifted up, they didn't understand that they had brought in the symbol of the plan previously embodied by the rehearsal. While Jesus' loved ones mourned at the sight of the tree thrown at his feet, he looked at the stake on which he was to hang and cried, "Father Abraham, indeed!"

After a resurrection, the seed from the overshadowing partner falls into a receiving place that incubates the seed. Protocol demanded that the stake on which Jesus hung at Calvary was to be erected before onlookers, who only saw a tree from which he was to hang. The true Vine was able to accept his mission, because he understood that the stake that was raised was the branch from whom he had descended.

In the rehearsal, Sarai, the tomb, received a salutation and a word from God through the mouth of an angel. She was called by a name contrary to her ability to bear children. Sarai could not have borne one child, much less a nation, but God called her "Sarah," the mother of nations of kings. After a word from the Lord, Sarai, called by another name, received strength to do according to the name she was called. Though she was dead, she conceived, as promised, and bore Isaac. In the rehearsal, the Word of the Lord, spoken through the mouth of an angel, called Sarai by another name, which caused her to produce. In the primary event at Calvary, the Lord himself changed the name of the tomb, and it mimicked Sarah. Sarah brought forth Isaac, and Emmanuel sprang forth out of a cemetery.

God wants to move upon anyone who says that his circumstances make it impossible to produce. Abraham presented to God a maiden who could bear children, but God was looking for the woman who was barren. Doing the impossible is God's signature that authenticates his work.

When Jesus was on the cross at Calvary and said, "Woman," the disciples thought carnally and took hold of Mary. Both the disciples and Abraham took hold of the wrong women. God is always for the woman who cannot bear fruit, so he can plant his seed, which is the Word of God.

Many women were familiar with childbearing, but when it

came time for God to bring forth the Son of God out of heaven and present him on the earth as the Son of Man, he looked for a virgin, a woman who, alone, could not bear a child, to confirm that the Son born of this virgin was indeed who Mary said he was. If God had chosen a childbearing woman, who was to say that the child was not her husband's?

Yet God did not choose Mary only because she could not bear, because every woman at some point in their lives can claim to have been a virgin at one time. I will not intentionally insult your intelligence, but certainly you know the difference between *abstinence* and *barrenness*. Mary was not barren; she was a virgin. It is just as impossible for an abstinent woman to bear without the seed of a man as it is for a barren woman to bear, even though she has been with a man. The surgical hand of the Lord had to move upon the virgin if he wanted her to bear a son. Therefore, God spoke to Mary, who had never lain with a man.

For the same reason, Jesus spoke to the virgin grave, where no man had ever lain, to do something that would otherwise have been impossible for either virgin (John 19:38–42). Both Josephs had to take a second seat to God's Son: Joseph, the carpenter husband of Mary, and Joseph, the counselor of Arimathaea, who begged for the body of Jesus and gave his tomb, where no man had ever lain, to incubate the Master for a few days. It is just as unnatural for a virgin to bear without the seed of a man, as it is impossible for a man to come out of a grave. So, out of both "women," with whom no man had lain, God would bring forth his Son by supernatural means. The first virgin, Mary, who had never known a man, brought Jesus into the earth. Later, Jesus came out of the second virgin, the grave, where no man had lain, and he ascended back to heaven. Neither of these virgins was fit, in their own abilities, to do what God wanted done, except by God moving upon them and speaking his Word. He had to make a move on both.

You may very well be in a place where you do not fit, and it will take a miracle to do what you have set out to do. If this is the case, you are a candidate for God to stamp his signature upon whatever impossible goal you have set or whatever grave you are trying to come out of.

Mary, alone and frightened, stared into the eyes of Gabriel and said, "I am confused. How can this thing be, seeing that I know not a man nor does one know me? How can I conceive from nothing?"

Gabriel smiled and responded to the damsel, "Be not afraid or dismayed, for I bring from the throne of God the Master seed that impregnates anything and causes it to produce by impossible means: the eternal words that proceed out of the mouth of the everlasting Father. God's Word impregnates anything it touches. If it were possible for two rocks to connect and have a family, their children would probably come out looking like sand, but when the Word of God and his Master seed like a master key that fits and unlocks any door goes into a rock that is unfit to be a well, that rock produces water according to the Word that was spoken into it.

By God's seed, which is his Word and not the seed of a man, a man child was conceived by Mary. God's Word could just as easily have caused the rock in the desert to breed bread instead of water, just as he could have raised up children unto Abraham without the sperm of a man.

Knowing this, the angel humbly replied, "I know you are a virgin, and it is impossible for you to bear, seeing that the seed of a man has not touched you, but eternal God, the Father of all, has sent in his Word the Master seed, by which all things produce and consist."

Mary concluded, "Let it be done unto me according to the Word you have heard." Nine months later, a virgin, with the help of a spoken word rather than a man, held a son in her arms. God's Word, spoken through any other mouth to any other recipient would have yielded the same results. Moses spoke God's Word to a rock. An angel spoke to Mary. Jesus spoke to the grave. Of course, the grave received a double portion: the spoken Word and the physical Word that entered her bodily. No wonder she did in three days what it takes most women nine months to do.

Whether God's Word is spoken by an angel to a virgin or by a man to a rock, when the words come out of the mouth of God, the recipient will produce the impossible.

Ms. Carry

Perhaps if the grave at Calvary could have spoken, it would have asked the man hanging on the tree the same question that Mary asked the angel. "How can it be that you expect a tomb to conceive as a womb does, that you may be born again out of me? I am not a woman, that I can produce a living man. I am unfit for this job, and surely I will miscarry this man. All bodies that enter my property never leave my land."

Nevertheless, as God did unto the virgin after Gabriel spoke God's words into her ears, so he did unto the ground after Jesus saluted and entered the grave. The tomb, Ms. Carry, received the Word on Friday; at midnight on Saturday, she went into labor; and early Sunday morning, she witnessed the coming out of the Word in bodily form.

The other women ran a good race to the cemetery to witness an impossible birth, because, of all recipients, the tomb was known for miscarrying men. But the women were too late. "Whom do you seek?" the disguised gardener inquired. By the time the women had made it to the womb of Ms. Carry, she had already done what everyone said the tomb could not do. Out of the abyss of darkness, the Son had come out.

Mary was an important contributor in the fulfilling of God's plan of salvation, but the cemetery was just as essential as Mary. Where would the world be if Mary had conceived and delivered, but this other "woman," of whom Jesus was to be born again, had miscarried the Son, as she had always done before, from the first Adam until now? It would have been an abortion the world could not afford. But even Ms. Carry, the grave, produced when she received the Word of God.

MS. FIRE

Don't be dismayed and lose your cool just because Ms. Fire is fussing, all flared up, and keeping up a mess. She is only Ms. Carry, the grave, wearing a different dress. Regardless of the form in which the grave presents itself, when the Word of God is deposited, somebody or something is going to come out.

"Didn't we deposit three bodies?" asked King Nebuchadnezzar.

"Yes, sire," replied the servants. "Three were cast into the oven."

"How is it possible that they walk around unharmed in the belly of the fire? And where did this fourth fellow come from, whom we did not deposit?"

This fiery hole had been meant to abort forever in her fierce belly the bodies of God's babies, but the execution chamber of Nebuchadnezzar, which had produced only the cremated remains of all the bodies thrown into her, had become just as confused as the king, wondering how had she turned from murderer to maternal, from burning bodies into birthing babies. King Nebuchadnezzar had thrown three boys into the fiery furnace to be consumed in the fierce, fiery tomb and to kiss eternity, but the Word had already gone into the furnace ahead of the boys and created a fire escape. What was meant to be their death bed became the bedchamber of the Bridegroom.

Wherever the Word is sent, spiritually or physically, that dwelling place becomes a birthing place for the everlasting, immutable, indestructible, universal seed of God. Regardless of the recipient's character, it will produce. Marvel not, then, that a fish produced a coin, which was not itself flesh that could come out of a fish. God has been trying to tell us no matter how unlikely it is that we will come out of an impossible, smothering mess that if the Word is sent into that place, we should look to be blessed. God, by his Word, is bringing us out.

In the book of John, Jesus said that when we speak his Word, he and the Father will abide with us for the purpose of securing the integrity of his Word, and they will cause the thing that holds us to spew us out of its mouth, according to the words of God spoken into it. I, like Moses, could not have told the great king Nebuchadnezzar how a thing could be set in the midst of a burning fire and not be consumed to a crisp, but I could have counseled the furnace and told her that it is very hard to swallow when a rock is lodged in your throat.

This hot mama was supposed to produce a triple funeral for three bodies, but because the Word was launched into the furnace, she misfired and bore living triplets from her womb.

At the end of the day, the servants went to the furnace to get rid of the remains, to pull out the charred flesh, ashes, and baked bones of the three boys. Shadrach, Meshach, and Abednego had about the same chance of coming out of that fiery furnace that a crack addict has of coming out of a crack house. Crack houses don't produce Christians; they breed crack addicts. But we aren't to give up on a situation just because it seems impossible.

A crack house should not birth Christians, and a fish should not spit money out of its mouth. A rock should not go into labor and produce water as if it were a well. This fiery furnace was not a woman that should be giving birth to men, but when the Word went in, King Nebuchadnezzar beheld the boys walking about in the fierce, fiery tomb like gods, without any manner of hurt as though the furnace had become a female giving birth. What of that?

If a crack addict is held captive in the crack house, and a son of God sends his or her word, repeated from the mouth of God, into the addict's world, shall not the crack house be broken like the rock that produced water? Shall not the crack house, like the fiery furnace, become like a pregnant woman whose time has come and produce from her belly a Christian? I do not say that the crack house is a woman who should be birthing Christians, but I do know that when it comes to the Word of God, everything regardless of how hard it is or what reputation it has can become a receiver and produce. Is there anything too hard for God? I say nay!

For the sake of a child, a drunk, or one held captive by cocaine, be a receiver of God's Word. When the master seed proceeds out of the mouth of the Almighty and enters a person, place, or thing, these captives shall be delivered and shall come forth from that tumultuous place as pure gold. Just as Shadrach, Meshach, and Abednego came out of the furnace, so shall a Christian come out of the crack house without even the smell of smoke on his clothes!

ALL ARE VIRGINS

"There are threescore queens, and fourscore concubines, and virgins without numbers" (Song of Solomon 6:8 KJV).

The rock in the desert, the fish on the bank, the water at the wedding, the mist in the heavens, and even the grave at Calvary. No one of these looked any different from the virgin, when God used them to produce something. It was just as easy for his Word to bring water out of a rock as it was for him to cause a virgin to bring forth a child. Nothing under heaven is exempt from producing the impossible, if the words of God go into it. Whether spoken or physical, if the Word goes in, it shall not return void. It will accomplish that for which the Word was sent, and the receiver will yield whatever the seed of God's Word has planted.

Does it really matter what the odds are against you? The place where you are looks no different to God than Mary's virginity. What were the odds that a child would come out of the womb of a virgin without the seed of a man? By the same reasoning, something good will come out of every misfortune or mistake, when the Master comes into that situation.

Ms. Stakes often breeds chaos, but when the Master is in the midst of it, every storm becomes peaceful. God often uses mankind to do things on our behalf, but even if people can't help us, God does not need them to deliver us out of our troubles. When the words of God are received by a jail cell, a crack pipe, a bourbon bottle, a courtroom, a hospital cell, a child, a husband, a rock, a fish, stones, or anything else you can name, something good is going to come out of it, despite impossible odds.

Water doesn't bring forth wine, but when the Word stepped in at a wedding, the water produced wine without the squeeze of a grape, just as Mary produced a child without the seed of a man. When the Word goes into something, don't expect God to work things out through ordinary or traditional sources or means. You waste time when you try to figure out how God is going to get you out. There are ten thousand ways that God can fix any situation, or he may have one way to fix a thousand problems, so don't waste your mind's time wondering how or when he will do something. Don't be weary in doing well. Pray without ceasing until you see fruit coming out of the thing you have sent the Word into. Nothing is excused from being a receiver; God can use anything to do the impossible.

When God's Word goes into anything, "none is barren among them" (Song of Solomon 4:2 KJV). Everything his Word goes into will deliver.

MS. B. HAVEN

The Word of God always knew he was coming out of Calvary's grave, for the Master had plenty of practice before that. In fact, Calvary was a lightweight compared to the untamed, tenacious, misbehaving graves he accosted before he met Golgotha.

"Master! Master! Wake up! Carest thou not if we perish?" The question proposed to the Master confirmed that the crew was in a tumultuous fix. After all the things they had seen Jesus do, their faith was still weak. The disciples were at their wits' end, because the tempest was at its peak. The wind screamed and hollered at the top of her voice, and tide was so high that the water broke into the boat after seeming to have touched the sky. Had somebody not awakened the Lord, the mouth of the misbehaving sea would have swallowed up his disciples, and they would have joined the countless others who had been digested and lost in a watery tomb.

Even after the Lord awoke to all the commotion, the abyss of the sea still insisted on an abortion, but the wailing wind and the waters of the sea echoed like the cry of the mother who has found her child dead in bed. The cries, however, turned out to be the symptoms of a travailing woman in labor, rather than the pains of a woman who has lost her baby. After the Word spoke "Peace!" into the storm, these labor pains disappeared with joy that a child had been born. The sea became as calm as a rested mother who has only threatened to miscarry her sons. The grave situation that intended to wash ashore a ship full of dead men's bones, turned out to be a beautiful baby shower for the sons who had been delivered. It was evident that the sea, instead of miscarrying, delivered, for not long after the Word spoke peace, the dark clouds of death rolled away and the sun came out.

Ms. B. Haven, like Ms. Fire, is but the misfit Ms. Carry, wearing a different outfit. Whether death comes as a fire or a flood, the Living Water always lifts a standard against it. Like Ms. Fire, Ms. B. Haven further affirms that Ms. Carry, in any form, is all washed up because of the Word of Life.

PART II
THANK GOD I'VE GOT A MOUTH

THE MASTER'S SUITE

"Thy lips, O my spouse, drop as the honeycomb: honey and milk are under thy tongue" (Song of Solomon 4:11).

That secluded place where you are now may seem like the end of your life. Though it feels permanent, it is only temporary lodging. When the Word goes in, that dead end becomes a throughway. One way or another, God is going to spring you out. That tomb is about to become a womb, and the morgue is but a mother!

If this next story had occurred in your town and your time, you would have witnessed the body of an innocent little girl, wrapped in the arms of a loving but horrified mother who was wailing a sorrowful note at the top of her voice in unison with the distant siren of an ambulance rushing to the scene. You would have seen an emergency team arrive and try to press through a concerned crowd gathered around the mouth of the morgue that used to be the little girl's bedroom. You would have watched them use their geared-up crash cart to send an electric shock through the damsel's pale, limp body in hopes of snatching her out of the tenacious, ruthless clutches of death.

Then you would have heard the annoying, redundant,

high-pitched sound that accompanied the straight line stretched horizontally across the lighted screen, the sight and sound of the modern-day machine confirming that the young girl was indeed dead. But after the Master said, "The maid is but asleep," that same lighted line would have been the first to celebrate the damsel's return to the living as it danced in a zigzag pattern, hopscotching across the screen to affirm that the bitter taste of death had gone, and the morgue had turned back into a suite!

"And the roof of my mouth like the best wine for my beloved, that goeth down sweetly, causing the lips of those that are asleep to speak" (Song of Solomon 7:9 KJV).

You might be thinking in the back of your mind, Good for the girl. She was fortunate enough to have the Lord in the flesh stop by her place. But how do I get him to work on my behalf, seeing that he is ascended from the earth and back in his heavenly place?

Relax. Help is still available. In fact, when you invite the Word into your place, you too can experience a world of changes on this side of the resurrection. Absence of physical presence does not mean absence of power. Regardless of the form in which the Word of God comes bodily or spoken there is going to be a birth when the Word is deposited.

Although it came in different forms, both Sarah and the cemetery received the same treatment. Sarah received the spoken Word, and the grave incubated the body, but both "graveyards" produced the same results. "And the Lord visited Sarah as he had said, and the Lord did unto Sarah as he had spoken" (Genesis 21:1 KJV). The Lord's body is at the right hand of the Father. My mouth is right under my nose. The whereabouts of the Word's body is out of my control, but I can control the words formed in my mouth, and even if his body is absent, I will receive the same result through the spoken Word.

The power that raised the Word bodily from the dead is the same power that quickened Sarai's dead body, long before the physical Word ever came on the scene. While we are in this flesh, speaking what is written, that same power is going to quicken our mortal bodies, even though the Word is no longer bodily present in the earth. Even though his body has ascended, we must not deprive ourselves of the written Word. Otherwise, how would we know what words to administer out of our mouths concerning our grave places?

If I needed ten dollars, it wouldn't matter to me if I received forty quarters or ten one-dollar bills. Either form of money would satisfy the need. If I can't have the Word present bodily, I'll take the written words of God, because my mouth can take those written words off the paper and put them right in the place where I need them.

If I had a chronic illness, and the doctor came to me and said, "I have the medicine to cure your condition, but I will have to administer the cure in capsule form," I would not deny myself life just because I prefer an injection and only oral medication is available. Either form of medicine will cure my ailment. We don't have the Lord's bodily presence, but we must not refuse the by-mouth method, because the spoken words of God are just as effective.

If I want to fly to another part of the country, and the plane that could take me there has already taken flight, I can't make the plane turn around. So why should I stand gazing into the heaven at the plane that has already left? Instead I find the next reliable transportation: a train. The physical Word has already taken flight, but "His word in my mouth is like fire, fire shut up in my bones" (Jeremiah 20:6). Get your train of thought on track, and get on board with the written Word. Your tongue is the ticket that will get you to the place you need to go. Life and death is in the power of the tongue, and everybody has a ticket.

That burial plot you've been living in is nothing more than a hole for you to bloom out of. Thank God for your mouth! That unfortunate abyss you're in is about to be a mother, even if she is a morgue. Remember that the fish was not an ATM until the Word was spoken into it (Matthew 17:27). Was it Jesus' physical presence or the words that came out of his mouth that brought Lazarus out of the grave? If his physical presence was the key, then why did he speak to Lazarus' condition three days earlier?

The bodily Word has ascended, but I still have a mouth. If you cannot talk, don't bother about this section of the book. But if you have a mouth, you are already equipped with what it takes for the same power that brought him out of the storm to perform in your unfortunate state. Even if you can't talk, Jesus is able to do far above anything that we can even ask or *think* according to the power that works in us (Ephesians 3:20).

BORN TO WIN

Don't you think it strange that the world was created by spoken words? Isn't it interesting that God created man with a mouth? Of course, man, like any other living creature, needs a mouth in order to eat or he can't live. But man is the only creature who has been given an additional mandate to use his mouth to speak the words of God as much as to eat food (Matthew 4:4; Job 23:12).

God's spoken words delivered people and things out of dark, dead places long before the Word came on the scene in the flesh. What else but a word from eternal God entered the feline café and put the ferocious diners on a twenty-four-hour fast in their own dining hall to save Daniel from being eaten alive? Daniel emerged without a single scratch from the flesh-eating grave.

From the very beginning, God intended for man to rule with his mouth. After all, man was created in the image of God. How could we be a reflection of God's image without a mouth, seeing that God created everything by his words?

So that man would not be preoccupied with the shape of God's image saying, "I wonder what God looks like" he gave Adam a physical body that mirrored God's form. But the image of God that man was designed to reflect was and is far beyond a shape of God's figure.

No one brings a race car to a race just because it has a beautiful body. Despite its strategic design, if the car has no motor, the shape of the body is irrelevant to its purpose, because the car has no power to perform.

God did not put Adam in the garden just to model a design of God's figure. Adam was also to be an icon of God's power (1 Corinthians 15:47). God had more interest in how man would resemble him in power than as a reflection of the way God looked.

Man is beautifully and wonderfully shaped in an image of God's figure, but we are also shaped and formed in an image of his power. Through faith, we understand that the world was framed by the words of God. In order for man to be a replica of God in *power*, God formed man with a mouth on his face.

It would have been useless for God to give man a mouth, unless the man's circumstances responded when the man spoke the words of God's power. So God did a test run on the powers in Adam. He gave Adam a nameless animal kingdom to see if the words of God spoken out of the mouth of a human reflected the same picture as when God spoke the world into existence.

While Adam ate from the fruit of the trees to sustain his physical body, the Lord God brought every beast of the field and every fowl of the air to him to see, not the image of God's shape (what God looked like), but what Adam would call the animals (Genesis 2:7).

The emphasis was not on the animals but on the reflection of God's power exemplified through words spoken out of the mouth of the very first man. This proved that the words of God, spoken by a human mouth, could produce the same image that God did when he spoke. In the beginning, "God said," and it was or became, or was conformed to what he called it. So Adam, being a paradigm of God in power, spoke, and whatever names Adam called the animals, those were the name thereof.

The fall of man did not delete, nullify, or condemn God's system or original intent for man to subdue the world by the strength of his mouth. Sickness, among other bad things that God did not intend, crept into the earth because of sin. When Adam broke the law of God's commandment by eating of the forbidden tree, the law of sin and death, along with its consequences, was added to Adam's challenges. Adam originally had to subdue and dominate creation without any challenges without sickness, disease, or the other bad things that gained unlawful entrance through Satan's deception and Adam's disobedience. The consequences of sin changed the way Adam had to deal with challenges. But those challenges still had to submit to the words of God spoken out of the mouth of a man, because that was the way God had created Adam to deal with the challenges of dominating the earth.

When man could no longer hear the voice of God from within because of Adam's disobedience, God directed Moses to write down his words so that man could continue speaking what he ought to speak to maintain the quality of life intended before Adam failed (Deuteronomy 30:1, 11–15). Why would God have Moses write the words we ought to speak, if the things we spoke to would not abide by the law. What comes out of God's mouth is principal law. No matter what law is in effect before you speak, let every law be a lie, if it speaks out against the words of God that you speak out of your mouth.

Once God's words are spoken, whatever law exists has to change its statement when on trial against the law of God. The law of gravity ate the dusty grave dirt that fell from Jesus' feet when he ascended into heaven after he had risen from the dead. If the law of gravity bows when the Word is exalted, the law of sin and death is just another constitution that bites the dust when God's Word in us is lifted up. If anything, including our thoughts and feelings, exalts itself against or ascends above what God says about us, God says for us to cast it off into the dirt (2 Corinthians 10:5).

WISDOM OF POWER

The whole earth environment where Adam was planted was a challenge to him, even before he sinned. God never meant for Adam to stay naked, just as he never meant for the animals to remain nameless, so God left some challenges by giving Adam something to subdue. The animals were clothed but had no names. Adam had a name but was not clothed. There were challenges everywhere. God did not name the animals, but he did clothe Adam with the word and wisdom of his power, so that he could subdue and dominate all the challenges he would face.

Just as man from the dust was shaped into an image of God, the wisdom of God was built into man's image so that man might have power to imitate God in wisdom. The imagination of man was meant to be the epitome of God's wisdom. That's why, when man looks at a whale, he imitates God and builds a submarine. When man looks, thinks, and meditates, his imagination runs wild, because the image of God in wisdom was formed in man's image on the day that he was created.

Looking around, thinking of ways to hide himself, Adam subdued his nakedness by the wisdom of God's power. After looking at the garment of a tree, Adam made a covering of leaves to clothe himself and his mate. But God had told Adam to subdue and to have dominion, meaning that Adam was to dominate everything he subdued. Leaves from the trees subdued their nakedness, but the garments of leaves were not God's best work for Adam, because it was not at a dominating level. The best of the wisdom of God's power to dominate the challenge of nakedness was not exemplified through the first Adam or the last Adam. However, God did have other designers on reserve to validate that the wisdom of God's power among men was at a dominating level in everything he did.

When Adam looked around the whole earth and said, "I have dominion, from the airways of the heavens to the waves of the sea," the eagle looked down at Adam and said, "Not from where I'm flying. You are not above me."

Thinking that everything was finished, the eagle, in his ignorance, further challenged the wisdom of God's power invested in man. It asked, "If you are the head and not the tail, why are you down there while I'm up here?" What the eagle didn't understand was that God's finish was Adam's beginning. God's first day of rest was Adam's first day of work.

In his pride, the eagle mocked Adam and soared up into the skies at top speed, maxing out at over a hundred miles an hour. "I can spot a speck on the ground from thousands of feet from the sky," he boasted. But on one sunny day a few years later, those great wings of the wind were baffled by a clash of thunder that roared past him like a flash of lighting and soared through the winds of the wild blue yonder. Sensing that there was no smell of rain or gray sky, he looked all around, wondering what had ruffled his feathers. Again the thunderous noise grew closer and louder. Finally he looked up in awe, and all he could say was, "oh my God."

"Oh, no, my eagle friend," Adam responded boastfully

from the seat of a 747. "It is not our God or the weather, but I can see how you made the mistake, because I am made in his image. It is only I, but I'm glad you see the reflection." Adam continued, "I am what God says I am, and right now I am above and not beneath. I have what God's says I have, and he said I have dominion. I'm one hundred times bigger than you, and I dominate you in speed. And as for sight, no matter how far you can see, you can't possibly see into tomorrow. But our God said that he would show me things to come. You have eagle eyes, but I have the eyes of God's understanding. Oh, eagle, do you see the domination?"

The first time men experimented with flying, they tried all kinds of strategies and failed time after time, but after being faithful to the idea, the *wisdom* of God's power kicked in, and man did just what God told Adam to do in the beginning: to have dominion over the fowls of the air. What I see the Father do, I imitate, because I am also shaped in an image of God's power in wisdom as well as in a figure of his shape.

When man subdued transportation on land, he did so at a dominating level. When the means of transportation was transferred from beast to vehicle, he subdued the strength of the beast by substituting a motor for power. He substituted wheels for legs and replaced the eyes in the head of the beast with headlights in front of the hood. He didn't have to feed it, but when it was fueled, it rolled farther than the legs of a horse could walk and moved faster than any beast could run. The mode of the vehicle dominates the role of the beast in every fashion.

WORD OF POWER

A simple truck and trailer created by man, something we take for granted, can transport a thousand times the weight load that any animal can carry. The *wisdom* of God's power is exemplified when man uses his head and meditates on ways to meet his challenges. Man makes the strength of an elephant look like the power of an ant. If he can do all of that just by looking at a thing and thinking about it, imagine the kind of weight the *word* of God's power has when man speaks in domination of a thing.

The *word* of God's power carries just as much weight of glory as the *wisdom* of his power. If man took the same attitude when he looked through the window of God's *word* as he does when he looks at objects through the *wisdom* of God's eyes, cancer would not look so big when exercising God's power by speaking. The wisdom of power, by which man built the submarine that dominates the size, speed, and intelligence of a whale, is the same power by which sickness and disease and other challenges are dominated when we speak. Man has no problem thinking of ways to create a submarine to dominate the seas, but he has a problem with the word of God's power when it come to sickness or disease. He will imitate God in the wisdom of his power by creating a whale made of steel, but let something as small as cancer steal his health, and he says not a word.

If you are awed by the latest technology (the wisdom of God's power), you ought to try speaking his word to the challenges that threaten the security of your well-being. See how much the word of his power will dominate that statement you just received from the hospital or that negative report from the bank. Until the wisdom of his power discovers a answer for cancer, Mark 11:24 (KJV) provides an excellent cure: "Therefore I say unto you, what things soever ye desire, when ye pray, believe that ye receive them, and ye shall have them."

Time after time, the last Adam demonstrated the strength of the word of God's power. "Peace!" he commanded, and the roaring storm was subdued. The storm did just what the animals did when they were brought to the first Adam. Whatsoever he called it, that was the name thereof. When the Master was told that his friend was dead, he knew that the word of God's power was so dominating that death could simply be called sleep.

Maybe we forget sometimes to consider that men are imitating the word of God's power by creating things through the wisdom of God's power. God uses the wisdom of his power through technologies so that man understands and builds up the power of his mouth.

Everything now, by the wisdom of his power, is voice-activated. "Blessed be His glorious name, and may the whole earth continuously be filled with His glory, Amen! and Amen!" (Psalm 72:19). We can lock and unlock, or turn on and off, just about anything now computer, car, house, doors, and lights by a simple spoken word, and yet we still don't get the picture. That sounds a lot like Mark 11:24, as well as Proverbs 18:24: "Life and death is in the power of the tongue."

What I see my Father do, I do. He created everything to respond to the mouth of a man, yet man still thinks he is doing something by the wisdom of his power apart from what God originally intended. We can't help but imitate the one we came out of, even when we aren't trying to, or when we don't know we're doing it. Do we think we are creating something by our own wisdom? There is no power except the power of God, and there is nothing under the sun that's new.

Philip asked Jesus to "show us an image of the Father."

Jesus responded, "Have I been so long with you, Philip, and you still don't see the image or the picture God is trying to paint? The words I speak, which ignite the power of God to move and perform, reflect the results the Father gets when he speaks. His mouth, my mouth. He speaks, and things change; I speak his words out of my mouth, and things change. Get the picture, Philip? The image of his power is what's important for you to see. If you want your world to look like his world, do what he did in the beginning to bring about all worlds, and his will shall be done on earth in your world as it is in heaven. This is the picture, he has been trying to paint for us from the very first man. It is how we resemble him in power: our speaking is just as important as being an image of God's figure. Otherwise, you will just have a form of godliness but not according to power." (See Hebrews 11:3.)

The power is the dynamite, and the Word is the match. We can't control the power we have access to, but we can control what we speak to initiate the power. Don't worry about whether the dynamite will explode. Your job is to strike the match. Open your mouth, and experience the explosion!

Just as it is essential to speak the Word of God to sustain the original quality of life God intended in our world, it is necessary to eat food to sustain our physical bodies. We think more along the lines of praying to God to change our circumstances, rather than taking responsibility for the power he has already written. God thinks more along the lines of us taking command and shooting forth from our mouths the ammunition that he has already given us (Deuteronomy 29:29).

We are waiting for God to speak. God is waiting for *us* to speak. We have not yet made the transition. If the words are God's, it matters little whose mouth they come out of. Food only sustains our bodies, but the whole world is sustained by the word of his power, and we have mouths to form words. He has the power to create life, so you form words by speaking, and he'll takes the words you speak and bring them to life.

Respect of Person

The animals did *not* adhere to their names just because of Adam. He just happened to be the first human present.

When the children of Israel needed water in the hot, dry desert, but the only source available was dead, dry rocks, God did not go back to the garden to get the same man who had spoken to the animals so that he could speak to the rocks. Moses was the man chosen for this task, but any man with a mouth would have sufficed, meaning that, if the situation had been reversed, and Moses had been in the garden, the animals would have adhered to the names by which they were called, just as they had responded to Adam. The speaker didn't have to be Adam speaking to the animals or Moses speaking to the rock.

I could choose to go somewhere in my own car, but that doesn't mean that another car can't take me where I need to go. Regardless of which car I choose, for whatever reason, any car with a motor would suffice. Despite the reason a particular man was chosen, God needed a mouth. Any man available at that time could have easily done the job, if God had so chosen. It was not so much the speaker as it was the person whose word was spoken that ignited the power that changed each situation.

Too often we get caught up in the man involved, but if every situation is all about the man, we are in trouble. Adam is gone. So are Moses and Ezekiel. But we who are left here on this side of the resurrection still face impossibilities. Some of us are intrigued by the idea of water flowing out of a rock. We shout about the manifestation, but we miss the message. The manifestation was not meant to show off the man Moses. Neither was this demonstration only meant to show off God's power. It was also for us to know *how the power is released*.

I too am excited about the water coming out of a rock. It is always great to hear a good testimony. But after the rejoicing is over, I want to know what the person did to get the hand of the Lord to perform on his or her behalf, especially if God is no respecter of persons. What was the significance of God demonstrating his power to everybody, if that power was not accessible to the audience to whom it was demonstrated? Why would God show off his power, if it was not accessible to his people? If the power is available to everyone, then everyone must have something that activates the power. Was the Scripture, "Man shall not live by bread alone but by every word that proceedeth out of the mouth of God," written only to a certain man or group or because a person was called to ministry? In fact, Deuteronomy 30:11–14 confirms that anytime God uses one man, it is not so that people will build a monument around the man, as though he has done something of his own power. It is to demonstrate to the audience the power that is available to all people.

If God is not a respecter of persons, then the man chosen has nothing more special than the rest of us to cause the hand of the Lord to move. Jesus spoke to a grave. Moses was told to speak to a rock. Ezekiel spoke to bones. All power points toward the mouth, not the man. God has never limited the performance of his Word to a certain individual. "If any group, even if there is only a couple of you that join forces, it is inevitable that anything would happen in the midst of us three when the two of you agree with me and speak what I have spoken" (MSV).

Our Master has ascended, but we still have mouths. Jesus used the same tool to bring Lazarus out of the grave that Moses used to bring water out of a rock. You may say, "Well, I spoke to the thing, and it didn't change." Is the *thing* telling the truth, or are *God's promises* true? Then keep rejoicing.

If someone promised you and me a million dollars, and you got your million that same hour, but I had to wait a few days, as much as I would wish that I'd gotten mine in the same hour, I wouldn't give up hope if I had to wait a few days. Every time I'd get low, I would remind myself to be patient. It might not come today, and it might not be here tomorrow, but at least I'd know it was coming, because God is not a respecter of persons. So I delight myself again, waiting faithfully for the time allotted by the giver for me to receive my million. In a month, I will be a million dollars richer, just like you.

RESPECT OF THING

The Word laid aside all godly power, came out of a spiritual dimension, took on the nature of a man, and stepped into the shoes of the first Adam not to walk by a new creed of power brought down from heaven with him, but to breed quality of life by the same system of power that the first Adam had neglected through disobedience to the end that he might give men a clear picture of how the first Adam and his heirs were to walk in power before God in the earth. The demonstration of God's power in the first Adam was short-lived; but the last Adam, being obedient, walked faithfully in the shoes of the first Adam, even unto death.

He also showed us that not only animals were to conform to the words of God spoken out of the mouth of a man, but that *all* things were subject to the command of men according to the power God invested in them. Storms conformed to the word of God's power, but not because of the man, for the man had already been present in the bottom of the boat. The storm did not shut her mouth until the man *spoke*. Moses spoke to the rock in the desert, and Ezekiel spoke to the bones in the valley, but Jesus had not even been present at those times. Whether the thing was a bone, water that was to become wine, or a grave, all things conformed to God's spoken words. The fact of the matter is that no thing is immune to change when it hears the words of God, and God is no respecter of persons or things.

You may not be in a hole because of your bones, but your bank account may be as dry as Ezekiel's bones in the valley. Who can restrain your mouth from sending God's words into the vault of a bank? If his word was accomplished in a valley full of bones, who says the bank is off-limits? His words, once spoken, shall not return void.

You may be broke, but the Word of God cannot be broken. If God's words goes into a thing, something is bound to happen. The person, place, or thing that is bound has to be loosed, because the Word of God is not bound. Whether the thing is a rock, a bone, a storm, or a neighbor, nothing is off-limits. Not even a mountain can escape the power of the speaker (Mark 11:23).

It may very well be that one of the reasons our souls are saved but our savings are lost is that, after Romans 10:9, we stop talking. If the Spirit followed the Word into my body and saved my soul, who says that the Spirit wouldn't follow the Word if I speak it into my savings? That same Spirit that quickens my mortal body ought to be able to put a fix on my bank, especially if I tithe. A grave is a grave, and dry is dry. If, every time you reach into your pockets, all that comes out is dust, that sounds too much like a graveyard for you not to speak up.

God is always willing to turn a graveyard into a garden. It doesn't matter if the words of God are released into a valley or a desert. Not only is God without respect of persons or things, but he is also without respect of place.

RESPECT OF PLACE

The Master confirmed that the words of God would work, whether sailing the high seas in the midst of a storm or on a stake out in the middle of a graveyard. By his word, Jesus proved that God's word works, even if you are abandoned in a desert.

You may not be in a desert, but maybe your health is the dumps, and you are destitute, confined to a bed in some room. Your bank account may be meaty, but cancer is eating you down to a skeleton, and your life is hanging in the balance by only a thread. Who does cancer think she is to put her mouth on your body? Does she not know that you have a mouth to speak Proverbs 3:8? If God, by his Word, went into a den to stop the mouths of lions from chewing up the bones of Daniel, he will come into that treatment center where you are, to stop cancer from making a meal of your body. "Let the sick say ...," and whatever you call it, that will be the name thereof.

Regardless of the conditions where the Word is sent, the Spirit is ever ready and prepared to take the power of God wherever God's Word is spoken. He was so anxious in the beginning to perform his creative duties upon the deep, that he moved in place upon the thing to subdue it *before* the speaker even spoke. The Spirit, by divine obligation, is anxiously waiting to perform wherever the words of God are spoken. "I hasten my words to perform it" (Jeremiah 1:12).

It's a Jungle Out There

If God went into a den full of lions to save a kingdom, he is not a respecter of person or place, so there is nothing so tenacious that it will keep him from coming where you are. Even if the temperament of your kingdom is that of a jungle, you can dominate and subdue where you reside.

If you proclaim to everybody that you are a blessed and highly favored king, don't move to the suburbs and leave your kingdom hanging out to dry. If a man lacks wisdom, let him ask God for it. If he lacks power to do the impossible, let him accept Jesus. If he lacks a kingdom to subdue, after Jesus has made him priest and king, let him stand on the throne of his front porch and look at the conditions of his domain (Revelation 5:9–10).

Even if your neighborhood is a wild place, you are not in some jungle where the Spirit will not come. If you are afraid as you observe your territory from the terrace of your palace, remember that you are not the first man God has ever placed in a wild kingdom and told to dominate and subdue it until it looks like a garden.

The poor conditions in the wilderness brought out the riches of God's wisdom in Adam. What good would it have been for Adam to have the wisdom of God's power if there was nothing to challenge the power in him? God put a garden within Adam, placed Adam in a wilderness, and *called* the wilderness a garden. Who said that the wilderness where God placed Adam was a garden? Did you forget that God calls those things that are not as though they are? If that wilderness was indeed the utopia or the garden of perfection that you and I have imagined in our minds, why would God tell the man to subdue a paradise? Sure, everything in the wilderness was in perfect condition, but who said the conditions of the place were perfect?

You may hire professionals to move you into a new house, but just because the place now has furniture doesn't mean it's organized. God's first day of rest was Adam's first day of work. The job of the professionals was finished when they dropped off the furniture, but your job is just beginning, because nothing is in the right place. When God said he was finished, he meant that the place had been furnished with everything it needed for the man to make the wilderness look like what he called it.

If the animals wandered around without names, it is likely that there were other things as well that needed attention, beginning with the nakedness of Adam.

Make no mistake about it: Adam was planted in wild conditions. Besides, what would you call being in the woods surrounded by a bunch of animals? He had no shirt for his back or hut to live in, so be careful of complaining about how little you have to work with, or about who will not work with you in the place where you reside. Remember that Adam was placed in his wild kingdom, alone, with no one to talk to and no friend to support him.

Adam didn't have a ride to work or a job to ride to, but it

wasn't long after being in the place where God had set him that God gave him a job. He didn't need transportation, for God brought work to him. He may not have had an iPhone or an iPad, but he had the eyes of understanding, and when the nameless animals met the naked man, they knew he was clothed with the wisdom of God's power when he started prophesying in that jungle. The power of God was so strong in Adam's voice that the animals, from the elephant to the ant, conformed to his words by answering to whatever name he called them.

What's in your world, king, that is challenging the power of God in you? The gang in Adam's hood had no names. Gangs in your kingdom may have names but no identity. It is highly unlikely that you will meet a lion running down the street of your neighborhood, but a drive-by shooting in your kingdom is just as lethal as a lion. AIDS is just as venomous as an adder. "I send you out as lambs among wolves," God said.

But that wild place will come together, wherever you are, because if God gave you power to tread on serpents, you have power also to subdue the wolf, the lion, the tiger, the bear, or whatever Goliath stands in way of your dominating and subduing your kingdom. Wherever you are, when you face the impossible, speak the words of God. The Spirit will follow that word into the place where it is spoken and rectify whatever thing is spoken to by the believer, because God is not a respecter of *place* any more than he is a respecter of things or persons. God planted the man in a wilderness, because the garden was in the man. So the conditions of the place where you are only tip you off to what's inside you.

The whole world lies in darkness, but Jesus said, "I am the light of the world." The darkness of this world is what brought out the light of the Son. And everywhere the Son shone, the light simply dominated the darkness. Where else would "the way, the truth, and the life" be sent, other than to a place where man, who had lost his way because he had lost his mind, was living in the midst of a grave?

God will send you to terrible place, because you have a tenacious anointing. The Prince of Peace is necessary in the midst of a storm. Everything you face in life is not happenstance. God brought the challenges to the man in order to put a demand on the power. There are challenges that come because of the law of sin and death, and then there are some challenges that God brings to your doorstep.

But God is still God, and his plan for man to dominate every challenge has not changed. Everything in the world is to be subdued into alignment with the quality of life God intended for us to live.

THE SPIRIT AND THE SPEAKER

There were three men who were neighbors. One neighbor had an air conditioner, but his power was off, and he was miserable because of the heat. The second neighbor, just like the first, was miserable because of the heat, for he had electricity but no air conditioner. The third neighbor had both an air conditioner and electrical power, but he suffered from the same heat as his two neighbors. He had all he needed to be cool, but he wouldn't turn on the switch.

If you have connected to God's power by accepting Jesus, you have the power in you that will change anything you speak to. However, though you are saved and connected to the power, if you are not speaking God's Word, you are just as unproductive as one who does not have the power of the Spirit.

Sinners have the power of the tongue, because they have mouths; but they have not connected to the power of the Spirit, because they have not accepted Jesus. You have accepted Jesus and are connected to the power, but if you won't turn on the switch, you are suffering from the same heat as the one who has not connected to Jesus, all because you won't speak.

The switch, the air conditioner, and the electricity, though they are three, are also one. This simply means that all three members need to connect, and once connected, the three become one unit of power that produces cool air. Electricity in itself is power, but it is dead to producing air without the air conditioner. The air conditioner is made to produce air, but it is dead to producing cool air without power. The switch without the air condition is just a switch, yet without the switch being in the "on" position, the fully powered air conditioner can't produce cool air. All three must be joined together as a unit, and none of them can produce air without the others. But once they are joined together, they become one: a powered, air-producing machine.

THE WORD, THE SPIRIT, AND THE SPEAKER

These three the words of God, a speaker, and the Spirit were designed, even before the beginning of the world, to be one life-producing unit.

The Father did not design one to work without the others. In fact, it was this unit each part fulfilling its particular function with the others that created all things. That system did not change just because Jesus, the speaker the Word, as he is called by name put on flesh and came to the earth. Because God is God and does not change, the Word connected right back up with the Spirit in the waters of the Jordan River after coming to earth not just to meet with John the Baptist, but to connect with God's power.

The Word and the Spirit meeting up at the Jordan was nothing new to either Jesus or the Spirit, for it was the Spirit that had, in the beginning, moved upon the face of the deep when he and the Word were getting ready to create the world.

Although the Spirit moved upon the face of the water, he did not perform or created anything in the depth until he heard from the speaker. Likewise, at the Jordan River, something in-depth was about to be done for man by the Spirit. He had already been dwelling among and moving upon men for some time now, but he had to wait for the speaker before he could start doing his in-depth work. To be productive, both had to work together.

The Spirit always stands ready to perform. He knows what to do, but he performs nothing until he hears God's words directly from the mouth of the Father or Jesus, unheard by us. If the Spirit performs in any way or makes any kind of move, it is in response to a speaker.

The speaker is vital. God could have made the bones in the valley whole without Ezekiel. The water came out of the rock when Moses hit it, even after he was clearly told to *speak* to the rock, which means that the water was already in the rock. God wanted the man to speak to the rock in order to teach man God's divine design of things. Whenever God wanted his Spirit to do something, the Spirit never did it without a speaker (John 16:13). Before the Spirit moved in with you, there was a word from a speaker (Romans 10:9). The words spoken must have, at some time or other, come out of the mouth of God. Even when those words are spoken by someone besides God, the Spirit honors God's words when he hears them.

A person must speak before he or she receives the Spirit. Therefore, the Spirit does not indwell you to *make* you speak, because you are already a speaker. Since you are the speaker, he indwells you to empower you, to bring your words to life. If there are no words, the Spirit, though he is in you, is powerless unless God, Jesus, or another spirit-indwelled person speaks on your behalf.

Just as an air conditioner, though it is plugged into the

electrical power, is powerless to produce air if the switch is off, the speaker's words must have come, sometime or other, out of the mouth of God. Needless to say, the Spirit is the power source. He requires a speaker, because the written Word does not have a voice, for words written on a page cannot speak. However, they were made to be spoken. This makes you, the speaker, a vital contributor if the written Word is to be effective. If the Spirit is to be effective, he needs to hear the Word, spoken out of your mouth, and "whatsoever He shall hear, that shall He speak" (John 16:13). This simply means that the Spirit and the speaker work as a unit to produce the desired thing that has been spoken.

We might not have the same mission as Moses or Ezekiel, but no mission is impossible if we have a mouth. You may not speak Hebrew, Arabic, or Greek, like Ezekiel or Moses or Jesus, but that's okay, because the Holy Ghost knows the words of God in any language. He will adhere to the words of God spoken out of any mouth of any man in any place. If God is in us, he is for us. If he is for us, who can be against us? You were born to win.

Speak the Word into anything in any language, wherever you are, and whatever it is will turn maternal and produce! "And there is not one that is barren among them" (Song of Solomon 6:6).

What awaited the Master after the cross was a place that aborted and never let any body escape. What the Master needed, before he was deposited in the ground, was a module that would give birth, an aperture that would release him. Therefore, he chose life and spoke into the grave which always declared, "Do not resuscitate!"before they planted him. He said to the grave, "Woman!"

Those who agreed with the cemetery and did not expect a return on their investment saw only a graveyard. But the Tree of Life knew that Jesus was the seed of Abraham and had the resurrection DNA (Do not abort!) in his genes. It was a graveyard, but three days later, when the Tree of Life sprang up, the garden confessed by manifestation that she had been converted. The grave was indeed a dead-end deal, but wherever the Word is invested, anything can happen.

It doesn't matter what kind of hole you're in. Peter witnessed the power of the Word when he followed Jesus' fishing instructions and came out better than when he went in. When he and the Master were without money, the Word sent him to the "Bank of Capernaum," and when he stepped on the banks of his fishing hole, money came out of a fish. When Peter was on his boat and found no fish for his business, the Master spoke, and the resulting load of fish broke the net and Peter broke the bank. In the first account, Peter obtained money for taxes. In the second, he experienced an increase in business.

If you have a mouth, that abyss where you abide is trembling right now! The Word of God, out of your own mouth, is springing you out of the mouth of that tumultuous place! It might take three days for that morgue to turn maternal, but wherever the Word is planted, there shall be a return. That abyss is no longer holding a helpless person who has no hope, because you have choice words from the Book of Life to plant with you in that place of death.

Never mind her hypocrisy, Ms. Carry is one of the longest-winded liars you will ever come across. She lied consistently for seventy-two hours, while holding the body of our Master. But a lie can only last for so long when it is pregnant with the truth. In the end, the truth always comes out, and the truth shall set you free!

What is truth? God's Word is truth, and you have a mouth to speak it! That tomb you're in is about to do the inevitable. When the Word of God went out, two virgins got pregnantMary and a graveyard. A fish spit out money. A mule got a promotion and start speaking words like a man. Lions stopped eating meat. The clouds started making bread. Water made wine. Blood came out of water.

If your situation is desperate, you don't have the luxury of waiting until you finish this book! Open up your mouth and drop the balm right into that dark arena of your life and expect nothing less than the impossible to happen!

Lazarus would tell you that the Word doesn't have to be bodily present for the power of God to rescue you out of a hole.

"Master!" Martha cried. "If you had been here, my brother would not have died." Everyone cried; the men wept upon their shirts, and the women wailed upon their skirts. Then Jesus also cried, but not because of the crowd, or because he was hurt, or even because Lazarus slept. Jesus wept because there is always a breaking forth of water before there is a birth. No one understood that he had sent his word ahead three days earlier, saying that Lazarus was not dead but was asleep. Then Lazarus, by the Word's power, was no longer dead in a grave. How sweet it is to know that when the Master checks in, death is no longer the end. Though all the signs say "dead end," God's Word is always true. Wherever God sends his Word, it never returns void.

Don't think that Lazarus' life was spared only because it was Jesus who spoke the Word of God. The life of a seer was saved by the speech of a mule. If the power of God, by his Word, works through an animal, then you as a person should feel really powerful right now. Man up! Without wrath or doubt, declare God's Word, because his desire is to the sons of men.

Open wide your mouth! If you speak into something, surely something or someone will come out of it. Wait for it.

PART III

WHERE'S THE BABY?

DADDY'S RESURRECTION

Nobody escapes the holes in this life that we inherited from the graveyard of Adam's disobedience. You would be surprised at the kinds of graves that used to enslave those of us who have become the sons of God, whom the Word of God has raised from the dead. It's not that we have never been dirty; it's that the Word does such a godly-good job of cleaning us up, because when the Word enters a life, he wipes the slate clean. "For ye are clean from the dust of whatever dirt you were into through the Words I have spoken."

Those of us who have been cleansed through the Word and have come out of a void now look as fresh and refined as the new money that came out of the mouth of the fish. We are all dressed up in our Sunday best Armani suits and designer dresses smelling as sweet as if we had innocently dropped out the window of some heavenly suite. We are no longer bitter, because we have been cleansed through the Word, which was spoken into that dead end we were drowning in. If only people knew what we were delivered from, if only they could have seen us while we were still dressed in our graveclothes, they would have thought they'd seen a ghost.

Before the Word washed away the graveyard dirt, we wouldn't have been caught dead in the places we are now. "Missionary Minnie" now works in the Lord's house and speaks for the Lord, because somewhere, sometime, God changed Minnie's mind. Like Saul, who was speeding along the road to Damascus in the wrong direction, Minnie was resurrected from her dilemma only after she met the Master. We'd be surprised at the dirt that used to come out of that missionary's mouth before her resurrection, and the kind of house she came out of. The good sister and reverend didn't always wear long dresses and speak in unknown tongues, for the language she spoke back then was quite common to man.

I thank God that the Word met most of us and washed the slate clean before we met! Jesus said that we are flesh of his flesh and bone of his bones, but I am not afraid to admit that I hope the skeletons never fall out of my closet, because back then, those bones looked nothing like the framework the Master has given me now.

There is a reason that "Deacon Joe" insists on standing while everyone else is praying on bent knees. The deacon is not putting on a show. He really is glad that God brought him out of the hole he was in, and the place that had once held him captive had insisted that people stand, even while praying.

My dad was bound and enslaved, buried in the bottom of a whisky bottle, but just as Moses took the Word of God into Egypt to bring the Israelites out of that tomb, a man by the name of A. G. Green stepped into my dad's situation. While the smell of alcohol was still on my daddy's breath, Mr. Green brought him the words of God in the form of a question.

"Stokes," he asked, "do you love the Lord?"

My dad laughed and said, "Man, what kind of question is that? Everybody loves the Lord. Why do you ask?"

"Well," the preacher said, "I read somewhere in the Bible that the Lord said, 'If you love me, you will keep my commandments.'"

"So, what's the problem?" my dad responded. "I go to church."

"So does the Devil," the preacher replied in a calm, soft voice. Slowly placing his right hand upon my father's left shoulder, he leaned slightly forward and whispered into my dad's ear, repeating the question: "Do you love the Lord?"

"Yes," Daddy replied, "I love the Lord."

The evangelist responded with confidence. "Jesus said, 'If you love me, you will keep my commandments.' And being drunk isn't one of 'em."

The belly of a whisky bottle produces drunks, but the Word went in and dragged Daddy out, and when Daddy came out, there was not even the smell of corn liquor on his breath. Only a few of God's words had been planted, but after the Christian was delivered from the bottle, another strange, amazing thing happened. An evangelist was born out of the Christian.

God is not finished with you. Your deliverance out of your dilemma was only the beginning of God's liberation. In fact, the reason you were resurrected was so that your potential could unfold and develop. God did not bring you out of the hole you were in just so you could feel free. That pleasant sensation will only last for a while.

"I am the vine, ye are the branches, and my Father is the husbandman," Jesus said. When you come out of whatever ground once bound you, the same hand that brought you out and comforted you is going to groom and prune you.

It saddens me that, immediately after our resurrection, we, the people, shout to high heaven about how God brought us out of what we used to be into. Instead of picking up the cross, we find a warm pew, because we don't know the next step for taking advantage of our liberation. Therefore, we never produce the potential that was hidden in us before our deliverance. It appears that every time God pulls something out of somewhere, his work is not finished. We have something stuck inside, and he commands that we bring it forth to contribute to something outside of ourselves.

In the beginning, the waters that were void and without form hung in space, and after God spoke, the earth emerged from the water. Then came the command for the dry land: "Earth," he said, "now that I have brought you out of the waters, it's your turn to bring something forth." Suddenly, out came the flowers, the grass, the trees, and all that exists in nature. Then came the man, and out of the male was delivered the "man" *w*ith an *o*pening for *m*anufacturing *b*abies, or *womb*.

Your deliverance out of whatever hole you were in is only the beginning. God did a work on the belly that dark place and commanded it to free you. Now it's your turn to do the impossible.

Ms. Sing U

17

"Whither is thy beloved gone? I am my beloved's and my beloved is mine. The king hath brought me into his chambers. I slept, but my heart waketh; My beloved spake and said unto me, Arise up, my love, my fair one and come away. The winter is past, the rain is over and gone, the flowers appear on the earth. It is the voice of my beloved that knocketh, saying to me, Open, the time of the singing of birds is come" (Song of Solomon 1:2–4; 2:10–12; 5:2; 6:1).

"Sing, O barren, thou that didst not bear; break forth into singing, and cry aloud, thou that did not travail with child ... saith the Lord" (Isaiah 54:1 KJV).

If, after many years, the church where you serve can only stir up the janitor in you, your church should be missing you, come next Sunday because somebody missed the point of your liberation. If you've been in the church for thirty years, and all you have to show for it is your faithfulness to an establishment or organization, something is missing. It's quite all right to find a position in the church, but we must come to understand sooner better than later and teach the children of the next generation that, after the Savior brought you out of your dark place, the church was meant to pour into you the right kind of word so you could prove what is that acceptable, good, and perfect will of God.

In truth, the world God delivered you from is missing you. However, the world you were born into has seen you take the Master's hand in marriage but has yet to record a birth after the wedding. What in the world is inside of you that made God pull you out from among so many imprisoned people? At every wedding I've gone to, the couple couldn't wait to get rid of the crowd so they could be alone. At the top of their list is the bedroom. Maybe that's why the bridegroom says that when you pray, go into your closet and shut the door, because babies are concieved in private places. Why come out of the mortuary from whence you were delivered, only to stand around in church as if membership and taking on a certain position are the final stage of your deliverance?

"A garden inclosed is my sister, my spouse; a spring shut up, a fountain sealed ... but thou maker, the God of the whole earth, who is thine Husband ... hath called thee as a woman forsaken" (Songs of Solomon 4:12; Isaiah 54:5, 7 KJV).

Wouldn't it be sad if you went to heaven, and our great God rewarded you for your service as an usher only to reveal that you had left shut up inside of you the cure for cancer? Wouldn't it seem like a waste that somebody had misunderstood why the wind of the Lord had blown upon you that night at church when you could hardly breathe for choking on your own tears? How tragic that no one recognized that something was supposed to follow your breaking forth with water. I agree that the church is a hospital of sorts, but you have been delivered out of the morgue and into the baby ward not just to say "goo-goo" over something that has come out of someone else. It's *your* time to deliver. *Your* hour has come. No woman goes to the hospital to deliver just water. However good you felt when you cried at the altar, it was not enough. Please, don't get sidetracked!

There are those Christians who believe that the "water" Jesus mentioned was the ability to speak an unlearned language after being born-again. Impossible! How could a man speak in a tongue he had never spoken before? Could a fish manufacture a coin? Impossible! Could human words roll off the tongue of an animal, after it received a word from God? Could that animal stand toe-to-toe with a prophet and hold a conversation with its master (Numbers 22:22–30)? Impossible!

Yet I have learned not to judge what comes out of the belly of anything that receives God's words. It is not mine to judge what gold might come out of the souls of those who are the heirs of salvation. For which is more common: the thoughts of a man rolling off the tongue of animal, or an unlearned language coming out of the mouth of a man? Both are impossible. You be the judge.

I've seen countless liberated people recycled back into the place from which they were set free, because they saw no purpose in their liberation besides being free from the abyss they were delivered from. They didn't know that the impossible was supposed to *continue* in them, even after their impossible liberation from their grave. God said that the day will come when he will pour out his spirit upon all flesh. When the hand of the Lord overshadows you, it is impossible for you *not* to do the impossible.

I submit to you that speaking with a new tongue is more than just "speaking in tongues." There are those among Christians who, when they received the gospel, were not inspired to speak any words other than "Thank you, Jesus" and "God is good." God is indeed good, and he is worthy of all praise. If the only evidence of a person's salvation is the tears that fall from their eyes, it is not my place to write them off as if they are not saved. How can I judge? The only evidence that the rock in the desert had indeed been touched by God was the running water that gushed out of its side. If people know that they were once bound but have been freed, then they are indeed alive now. Who am I to say that they have not been grafted into the holy vine and revived, just because they didn't speak in a language like mine?

My question to the tongue-talker and the tear-dropper is this: where is the baby? "A fountain of gardens, a well of living waters, and streams … Awake, O north wind; and come, thou south; blow upon my garden, that the spices thereof may flow out" (Song of Solomon 4:15–16 KJV). The breaking forth of water signifies that the hand of the Lord is upon you, but something should follow your water, be it tears or tongues. You've seen the water, the sign of impending birth, but have you identified the body that is to follow?

After there is a breaking forth of water, look for a baby. After God removes you from whatever has trapped you, he tries to extract from *your depths* something that he wants you and the world to see.

God induced labor on a four-hundred-year-old pregnancy, conceived by artificial insemination with the seed of Abraham in order to keep a promise God had made to a ninety-nine-year-old "tomb." God planted Joseph, Abraham's seed and great-grandson, in the belly of Egypt. God performed a C-section through Moses to extract from that pregnancy Saul, David, and Solomon because God had promised ninety-nine-year-old Sarai that he would bring out of her dead body a nation of kings.

Long after Sarah was gone, God still kept his promise. He led the children of Israel into Egypt, a nation of tombs, only to birth out of that dead nation a nation of kings. The water sac of the Red Sea broke, parting to either side, and a million-plus people came forth out of the belly of Egypt as one body after the breaking forth of the waters. The pains of labor came as a signal that the time for the birth had come. Pharaoh fell right into God's plan when he tried to abort the exit of the children by increasing their labor, for he didn't know that the pain he inflicted was a signal to the children that they were about to exit the body of Egypt. God showed Pharaoh and the Israelites all kinds of signs that it was time. He mingled blood with the water supply to signify that this was a birth situation and that the time had come for the exodus of the child.

Have you ever seen or heard of a baby being born where only water was present? Neither have I. After the breaking forth of water during a birth, there is always a show of blood. When our Master met the John the Baptist, he found him standing in water. That was why Jesus met John at the Jordan River. Three things must be present for a birth to take place: the water, the blood, and the spirit of a man, lest the unborn be born dead.

An unborn child can be fully formed in the womb, but if there is no spirit at the time of birth, the child is stillborn. John had the water; Jesus brought the blood; and the Spirit of the church the Holy Spirit descended like a dove upon the shoulder of love, lest the church on the day of Pentecost be found without life.

If there is no birth without a breaking forth of water and a show of blood, how can anyone say that the Master was birthed from the grave? God knew that the grave was dusty and could not provide either, so he went before the grave and produced both while hanging on the cross.

God signaled to Pharaoh that the head (Moses) had assembled together with the body (the children of Israel), and they were ready to exit Egypt, because this pregnancy, according to God's calendar, had come full-term, and the water of the Red Sea had to break.

By no means am I saying not to speak in tongues or cry tears. But something supernatural causes the water to part to either side, and there should be a birth from us after the breaking forth of water, lest we become just a "placenta" occupying a pew.

From the day that Adam sinned, the new birth process was already in motion. When we look down through the lineage of Abraham's loins, we see Jesus bearing the blood; but before Abraham, there was a breaking forth of water. Noah brought the flood, and Abraham followed with the blood. Salvation has always been about birth and production. Thank God that he didn't give up on the earth just because Adam committed suicide. The Father didn't just come up with the new birth plan when Jesus came on the scene. The minute the first Adam put us in a grave, it was ordained that we be born again.

Why did the Spirit of God move upon you? If you feel the urge to cry or the unction to speak, cry on, but on the other side of your waterfall, the world awaits that precious, good, and godly treasure that Jesus went into your grave to save. Since God induced labor upon whatever grave used to incubate you, and your water has broken, we long to see what product God wants to introduce to the world.

"Eyes have not seen, nor ears heard, nor hath it entered into the heart of man, the things which God hath prepared for them that love him, but he has revealed them by his spirit" (2 Corinthians 2:9).

Ms. Understanding

Before I was even a teenager, my family went to a tent revival. Most of the time, I and the other boys my age would find a place outside the tent to wrestle and play around, and when it was time for the altar call, we would find some way to get around going to the altar. But on this particular night, I didn't want to hide. In fact, I was kind of anxious to go.

When I went to the altar that night, a warm sensation went down past my head and into my throat. All I know is that it had a nice, smooth warmth, like a glow that satisfied my soul. But before it finished doing whatever it was going to do, they closed out the altar call. I hoped they would sing just one more song, or that somebody would ask, as they so often did, for the audience to say amen. It seemed at that point like anything would have set off whatever I was feeling.

I remember the warm tears rolling down my cheeks. I wanted so badly to shout, "Thank you, Jesus!," but I didn't want everybody to stare at me, so I just enjoyed what little there was of whatever it was upon me. Nevertheless, I knew that something had happened.

The strangest thing happened the next morning when I awakened. I grabbed some paper and a pen and started writing poems, one after another. The other thing that happened was that I started drawing different ideas that just kept pouring out of me even dreaming about certain things that had not yet been invented. Had I known that it was not a waste of time to pursue these ideas, had I known that the ideas were not a just a child's foolishness but were the babies God was revealing, I would have been persistent and finished what God had given me.

One of the ideas was for springs placed in the soles of footwear. After I drew it out, I thought, *This couldn't be from God. He doesn't want me wasting my time on this kind of thing. I should be praying or fasting or doing something more spiritually constructive, like going down and cleaning the church.* Surely God would appreciate me cleaning his house rather than wasting time sketching a shoe with springs. Little did I know that this was one of many babies kicking and screaming to come out of me. After a couple of days, I talked myself out of it altogether. I remember thinking that the idea was stupid anyway, that people would laugh me out of the room.

Can you imagine how shocked I was when I walked into a store some twenty-five years later and saw the same thing I had drawn as a boy sitting in my parents' living room? I couldn't believe my eyes: a name-brand shoe with springs.

I had missed out on things that God had impregnated me with. Because of my misguided belief that he only cared about my soul, I didn't seek what he had planted in me. The shoes were only one of many ideas, and it seems that God has purposely let me run across all the other inventions that I'd thought were a waste of good spiritual time.

We think that the more we go to church, the more pleased God is, but let me ask you something. How close can we get to God? And once we get really close to God, what is supposed to happen? Are we just to enjoy his presence, as we so often do, without knowing the purpose of his visits? Or are we to usher in his presence to get a clearer picture of his purpose? The plan of redemption did not negate God's original intent for creation. The redemptive plan was an additional task, added only because of Adam's disobedience. God had invested too much to wipe out the original plan just because Adam acted carelessly.

"What does it profit a man to gain the whole world and lose his own soul?" was not a cliché to induce a man to go to church, gain his soul, and neglect the world he was created to subdue. When God tells you what's really inside of you, you, like Sarah and Abraham, might laugh at the impossible. But whenever God tells you to do something, his hand is already upon you to do the impossible, even though you might not understand it. If he tells you to do something, there can be no doubt that the ability to do it was already inside you before he called on you.

When God told Adam to subdue the world that God had placed him in, he already knew that Adam, being one man, could not subdue that wilderness by himself. He didn't expect him to. But the men needed to accomplish that task were inside of Adam. Can't you just see Adam telling God that he needs more men? There was Eve, fresh off the wire, perfect in body, brilliant in mind, healthy as a bull, fertile as a jackrabbit, walking around picking lilies and Adam was talking about needing more men.

I'm telling you, your deliverance should escalate into more than just a shout and a cry. You've experienced all the symptoms of birth, but has anything come out of you since then besides tongues or tears? God miraculously delivered you out of the grave to do the impossible in you. "Shall I break open the grave and bring you into the church and not cause your water to break? saith the Lord. Shall I cause the water to break after you have been born again and then shut the womb? saith the Lord" (Isaiah 66:9).

After Saul met the power of God, out came Paul. Since when does an apostle emerge out of an assassin? It's impossible! Saul was an intense researcher of other men's material, and he was a serious pupil of foreign languages. But however fluently he spoke the many tongues he'd learned, there was one tongue that was unknown to him, one that he did not access until he met Jesus, the Word of God. After that access, Saul spoke in a tongue that he had not been taught in school. Impossible!

The Spirit moves upon you, and you come face-to-face with the thing that keeps you from the Savior, but there is still something inside of you that has not been discovered. Whether you are an apostle or an astronaut, just because you are accomplished in something does not mean that we have seen all that you have to offer. Just ask Paul. Even if you are talented enough to have made millions of dollars as a comedian before meeting Christ, we would be blown away by the gold mine hidden inside you *after* the Spirit moves on you. Your talents and gifts before Christ are only your face cards, and all you have shown us is the joker. But when the Spirit moves upon you, it is for the king that is still buried deep. Until the Spirit moves upon you and pulls the king and queen out of the deck, there remains a kingdom inside you, still in the ditch.

Ezekiel could run, but after the Spirit moved upon him, he outran chariots. Impossible! The student Saul didn't know that he was really searching for Paul, but when that eloquent orator and author met the Word, out of him were born the epistles that Saul never knew existed.

When the Spirit comes into your life, things should come out of you that you could not have produced until he moved in or upon you. Before the Spirit's power moved, Saul knew nothing about Paul. Until Saul looked into the eyes of the blinding Son, Paul couldn't see who Saul really was. If the Word could enter a donkey and cause it to speak human words to deliver a blind seer out of the hands of death, God can use you. If God used Paul an assassin, of all people to do a work or deliver a word, he will use you. You have not done what Saul did persecuting, prosecuting, and executing the church. But God used Paul, whom Saul knew nothing about, to spread the gospel over the isles, so that the blinded eyes of the Gentiles would be opened to Jesus.

What is our generation in for? God wants to finish the work that he began in you at the altar. Your water broke, and that night, you left the church, choking on your tears, because the surgical hands of the Lord were upon you! Know that he did not overshadow you for naught. The tears that fell from your eyes may not have been the cure for cancer or the answer for a fallen economy, but make no mistake: they were a solution for something.

When the Word of God met a frail, lonely, blind man on the outskirts of town where there were no doctors or modern medicine, he spat into the dust of the ground. The mixture of soil and saliva looked much like mud to bystanders, but the recipient leaped up and down, calling out colors, whirling around, and counting trees. Finally, exhausted from praising God, he bowed down to worship at Jesus' feet. Afterward, he walked by sight without the aid of a stick, telling outsiders that the mud had become a salve for the blind.

You don't have the luxury of being nothing or the privilege of feeling sorry for yourself because of the things you have suffered. Life may have dealt you a dirty hand and caused you to be hardcore and bitter, but God's hand is upon you now, and he still knows how to bring sweet water from the bitter core of a hard rock. Everything is a receptor, and nothing is excused from being used by the Master. The Word used the very thing that had been trampled on, spat upon, and counted as nothing to open the eyes of the blind.

Even broken bread that falls from the Master's table in

the Father's house are stones used to crush the enemy. "In my Father's house are many mansions," Jesus said. Inside of every mansion are many rooms. Right beside the Master's suite is a potter's chamber. This is where he takes crushed people, mends their broken hearts, and uses broken parts to make masterpieces. That's why the Master looked beyond your behavior and, despite your faults, bought you with a price. Precious stones are often thrown away as junk by those with an untrained eye. You are the Master's son, no matter how low to the ground you have stooped or what you've done. It was the Master who went down into the deep and rose out of the dirt to pull you out of the dust. No wise merchant wastes time getting dirty unless the dusty thing he got dirty for possesses some type of value. Therefore, you are a candidate for the Word to use as a cure for something. You are not so crumbled, trampled upon, or good-for-nothing that you are not meet for the Master's use. You are not prevented from eating at his table just because you have done bad things. In spite of your bad decisions, Jesus has said, "My thoughts toward you are good. I will withhold no good thing from you."

It took a miracle from God for a donkey to do what comes naturally to a man. You may not be an angel, but don't feel bad that you are a mere man. You could very well have been born an animal. If an animal did the impossible after the hand of the Lord came upon him, what are you kicking up dust about? "For the day shall come and now is, that I shall not be upon you, but in mankind."

We, as sons, are always wailing that we don't know what God wants us to do. Well, if it takes a miracle for others to do something that comes naturally to you, stop and get a clue. Instead of finding a comfortable pew, take a long look around you and see what other people go to school for, pray for, or struggle to do. If it comes naturally to you, get hot! And it could very well be that you have three or more talents buried. "All shall bear twins," so we know that we all have at least two talents.

And yes, we were created for multitasking. As fast as time passes, the mastermind behind it all did not afford you the luxury of mining someone else's treasure. So, be about the Father's business and mine your own treasures, to which you were called. There is a valuable thing in you, and I, for one, cannot wait for you to deliver your discovery. "Enlarge the place of thy tents, and let them stretch forth the curtains of thine habitations; spare not, lengthen thy cords, and strengthen thy stakes; for thou shalt break forth on the right hand and on the left" (Isaiah 54:2–3 KJV).

When the hand of the Lord moves upon you, the purpose of his visit is to expose and bring out of you the thing that was planted in the depths before you were born. No one was born to do nothing! If you have nothing to give, then it's time to meet the Master. "That if thou shalt confess with thy mouth the Lord Jesus, and shalt believe in thine heart that God hath raised him from the dead, thou shalt me saved" (Romans 10:9). And you, being void, dead, and empty, with nothing to offer, he will not only deliver but will cause you to deliver (Genesis 1:11).

Ms. Staken

"I have seen servants upon horses, and princes walking as servants" (Ecclesiastes 10:17).

When the day of Pentecost came, the Holy Ghost filled the room where the disciples were sitting, and when they all spoke in other tongues, those who stood by said, "They are drunk."

But Peter stood up and said, "You say they are mad because you can't explain the impossible. They speak in a language that they do not know, and you don't know how they do it. This is what was spoken by the prophet Joel: "In the last days when I pour out my spirit, even the eyes of the handmaiden and the field hand shall see something in a new light that they have never seen before. They too will speak forth and prophesy."

This means that God will give the employee something more meaningful to say than just, "Yes, ma'am" or "No, boss." When the Spirit moves upon a person, it is for neither cool chills nor hot flashes. Feeling good is only a side effect and a sign that the hand of the Lord is present to begin a new, good work in you, to uncover what was buried so that you can see beyond the scope of where you are.

God took the time to specifically reveal that the Spirit was poured out upon the employee as well as the employer, the handyman as well as the headmaster. Sometimes your vision, goals, and dreams are obscured when you abide under the covering of another.

Just because you are a handyman doesn't mean there's nothing in you to discover. The biggest mistake we can ever make is to mistake duty for destiny. Although the vision is far off and the dream seems impossible, it behooves you to find cover under the hand of the Lord.

Always remember that even if you hold the highest office in the building, if you are not the owner; you are still a servant. Owners have a way of creating comfortable spots for good servants, but all my life I have been told that good followers makes excellent leaders. If you are as good as you're paid to be, why not become part owner? But others can't look beyond the veil of the master's hand to see you as more than anything but what you are presently. You do so well as a servant, that others begin to think you were born to be nothing more than a servant, that you could never be a "king." They laugh to hear you say you are a king, because your kingdom is but a dream and a vision within the dungeon of your own mind. Unbelieving onlookers have eyes, but they can't see. To them you are, and always will be, only a hand.

Let people talk. It is the hand of the Lord speaking within you. People think you haven't made progress, because they can't see what you believe. They see you only as a servant. They don't know that because the hand of the Lord is upon you, you are presently a headmaster working as a hand. The place where you are planted feels more like a grave plot than a place for a plant to grow; the delivery room, where you are to deliver, looks more like a chamber of death than a place of birth. You were happy when God did a work on the grave and made it do the impossible for you, but now that it's your turn to come out of your comfort zone and do what God made the grave do, will you also rejoice in your labor pains until he brings something out as when you came out of the grave? Or will you quit in shame because people laugh at you and mistake you for less than you are?

You laughed at the hole you came out of, and you should have, because you were set free from something that others died in. Knowing that Sarah was a grave, Ishmael laughed at her when Isaac came out of her. I don't believe the lad was laughing at the woman but was simply amazed at the wonder of it. Sarah herself couldn't believe what God had told her: that she would, in her old age, bear a son (Genesis 18:11–14). Even after she had done the impossible, she couldn't believe her eyes, and she laughed again (Genesis 21:6). Abraham also laughed at the impossible that God was about to do (Genesis 17:17).

DANCING WITH KINGS

Make no mistake about it. When you get ready to do what God made the grave do to you, expect people to laugh at you, just as you laughed at the grave. Agree quickly with your adversary, because "a feast is made for laughter." Even though others think your feast is a funeral, keep rejoicing, and you will have the last laugh. Stop trying to look like a king in the making of your dream. God intended for you to look like you are losing, and those who mark and meddle while you're in the middle of your metamorphosis will serve you when you are promoted to king.

Before the worldwide flood of Noah's day, water had never fallen from the sky, for the water that moistened the earth came out of the ground. When Noah told the people around him what God had told him, he might as well have been speaking in another language. They laughed him to scorn, because he spoke of something that was coming that the earth had never seen before. They considered this old man and his sons to be insane, because, in the history of the earth, it had never rained. Noah's message, as well as the project God had given him, were mistaken for an old man's foolish dream, good only for entertainment. People laughed until they cried and called old Noah crazy.

It wasn't until the pretty, blue sky turned dark, the first clap of thunder rolled, and the last animal stumbled onto the ark that they wondered and said, "Oh my God! That old geezer wasn't speaking Greek after all. Now we're the ones floating up the creek without a paddle or a prayer!"

God said that he was going to give you a new tongue after you were born again. You may look like a donkey, telling folks you're a king while you're in the dungeon, but as long as you know where God is taking you, let the others laugh on. "A feast is made for laughter, and wine maketh merry" (Ecclesiastes 10:19).

To the prophet, his donkey looked like nothing more than a donkey, as long as it was carrying people's loads and chewing hay. It was only after the hand of the Lord moved upon the animal that human words rolled off its tongue. Then the prophet came down off his high horse and had respect for the impossible and for what the donkey had to say. You are only wasting your strength and time, trying to convince others of who you really are or trying to pour something new into old bottles.

Most of the time, your vision looks to masters, brothers, good friends, and others like nothing but water, but just because things are not clear to them doesn't mean you stop moving forward. Sometimes it will seem, even to family, that where you are going and what you are doing is just a waste of time. While they see water, you are tasting wine, so expect minimum support from them. Those who are blind to the impossible may think that you have lost your mind until they see the color of the wine. Continue serving well so well that others think you were born to do the task you have attached yourself to because God will use a master to walk a mile in a servant's shoes. But you, master, must never become so comfortable riding upon the servant's horse that you forget to walk like a king.

Joseph's brothers taunted him: "Here comes the dreamer. Tell us, little brother Joseph, what will it be today? Did you come to tell us another one of your wild and crazy dreams, or is this the day we all bow down to you as king?" Even Joseph's father, Jacob, who really loved his son, knew that something was happening, because Joseph had been born out of a barren woman. Jacob knew that the hand of the Lord had moved upon his barren wife, and although he knew not what was on God's mind concerning the boy, he knew that there was something special about this dreamer. Not understanding the visions Joseph described, Jacob asked him what it all meant. "Am I, your father and your brothers, who are all older than you to bow unto you as you saw in your dream?"

Stop telling your dreams to others who can't see your vision, especially kinfolk. If you know they don't see what you see, you just have to keep moving and know what you know. Most of the time, you don't altogether understand what you have seen yourself. Even if others understand what you have seen, there is still the probability of jealousy, which blinds people's minds, and they will be the last place you'll find help.

Because of jealousy, Joseph's brothers could not see past the dream to even consider that it might one day become a reality. So they put Joseph in a pit in a deserted place, not understanding that the place where they buried him to rot was the exact spot where God intended for the dreamer to be planted and grow. To the brethren, it was the death of Joseph's dream. To God, it was the beginning of his destiny. The brothers marked Joseph and stripped him of the coat of many colors that his father had given him, but later Jacob beheld his son Joseph, as one alive from the grave. And when Joseph came out of the grave, father and brothers all fell to their knees to kiss his feet.

Employees are necessary, but you are only a temp in training. Never mistake a job for a purpose. "I have seen servants upon horses riding as king, and kings in the earth walking as servants." This means that you could be king of the hill, with all its benefits, but when it comes to purpose, you are still a servant enslaved to a job. A king lives beneath his means and abilities because of one of two things ignorance or wisdom.

The posture of the king who doesn't know he's the king conforms perfectly to that of a servant. He lives beneath his means because he assumes, in his ignorance, that he must be a servant, because he is not yet positioned on a horse. He doesn't understand that his present position is not permanent, that he just going through a process.

If a prince understands the concept of the test, he retains his royal posture and, humble in his wisdom, temporarily takes on the form of a servant. But his posture is permanently fixed to that of a king.

After you are born again, you cannot take your walk with God at face value, for he said that, once we are born again, we are kings. A child may be a king, but if he cannot bear thorns, he cannot manage a throne. Therefore, though we are kings, we become students of governors, tutors, pastors, principals, and deans. But though we are in school, we must not forget that we are training for a higher position. So don't sweat it. Your dream is not in jeopardy just because you are positioned in a basement, working in the mail room.

Joseph's brethren planted him in a hole to drown his dream. But the divine husbandman used the hole as a pot to grow and groom a king. Follow your dream, but know that on your way to your destiny, not long after you've started your journey, there is a dungeon. For he that ascends must first descend, and low places along the way are necessary. Every king needs to know the operation of his kingdom from the ground floor to the round table on the top floor. If you exalt yourself to the top floor, you will surely fall to the basement, because you don't understand the foundation.

Joseph's brothers buried him in a hole to die all alone, but God planted him to grow as a tender plant that would sit upon Pharaoh's throne.

If you take things at face value and accept where you are now as your destination, you will remain in a hole every time, whether it's a college classroom or the mail room in the basement of a corporation. When a prince knows he is on his journey to become king, it is dangerous for those around him to underestimate him just because he is in servants' clothes. Divorce court is filled with people who took things at face value. Somebody is stranded on the side of the road right now, waiting for a tow truck, because he took things at face value. Goliath is dead because he didn't bother to do a background check on a king-in-training who looked like a sheepherder.

There was a king inside David who was just as deadly as the giant Goliath. David ran to kill the threats that others would have run from in fear, but because the king's warriors didn't recognize that the boy had a feel for battle, they wouldn't let David even go near the battlefield.

Jesse and his sons knew that Samuel was the authentic "eyes of Israel," and David's family had watched Samuel anoint David as king. Then his father and brothers had carried on with the business of the day. Although they never stopped treating the newly anointed king like a kid, the lad wasn't fazed. He kept writing psalms and giving God praise. As it was in David's case, we cannot always count on kinfolk to support what's inside us.

Because David's family didn't understand what was inside the lad, they sent him back to the pasture to herd sheep, dance and sing, and practice his craft with only a rag and a string. Perhaps on the back side of that mountain, alone, he shed many tears. But because they wouldn't let David rumble with the Philistine champion for fear the kid would stumble, David declared war on all giants and slew everything in his path that looked like on eincluding the king of the jungle.

One day, they finally let David loose to go to the battlefield with food for his brothers, but he knew why he was really being sent. He had a strong feel for battle and was attracted to killing giants. It was his debut as a top gun, his date with destiny, and the fight with the Philistine giant was the main event.

At five feet nine, the kid didn't impress his own family, much less others, as significant until he did the impossible and took the top off a nine-foot-five giant and brought his head in, as promised, on a platter.

Goliath, the giant, saw only a kid with a sling. Sadly for him, he didn't know that he was dancing with a king.

Dance, David, dance! Just because you're standing in your own tears, the spot you're in does not spell defeat. Praying always and not growing faint in that hole play a major role as you travel the road of your destiny.

Onlookers watch to see if your ship will sail or your feet will slip, but don't you be phased by what others think. It's not your fault if they don't know the difference between a slip and a praise, and your boat is not sinking. Now and then, every ship that's sailing the high seas takes a deep dive in the waves. But regardless of what outsiders think or hope to see, everything that's standing in way of your destiny will soon know that it's been dancing with a king.

Dance, kid, dance! Dance like David did!

I know Jesus said that his yoke is easy and his burden is light, but you know as well as I do that it sometimes seems like you are carrying the whole load as you shuffle along. The road ahead seems to get longer with every step, the load feels like a pound is added with every foot you travel, and you're hanging on by only a thread. Some nights, praying with all your might as you dry your face with a tear-soaked cloth makes you want to take flight. It seems as if Jesus is just standing by, watching you fight, and he's not going to help.

But the puddle of tears beneath your feet is not defeat. Jesus said that the battle is already won. So you just cry on as you cut a step and dance, kid, dance! The race is not given to the fast or the strong, so sing your song, walk on your tears, and dance through this storm.

By the way, congratulations. Run and tell your peers that you have just passed your beginner's class: *Walking on Water 101*. You've done the impossible, just stringing along. In spite of the threats and hanging by a thread, you've made it through the test.

And before you walk into your kingdom, don't forget to say, "Lord, thank you for the thread."

Printed in the United States
By Bookmasters